Grade 3
Poetry
Comprehension Skills

Contents

Introduction 3

Teacher Resources
Standards 5
Glossary 6
General Assessment 7

Unit 1: Teacher Resources
KWL Chart 9
Concept Web .10
Graph 11
Venn Diagram 12
Step Book 13

Unit 2: On the Silly Side
Lesson 1:   April
               by Anonymous
Teacher Information 14
Poem 15
Assessment 16
Vocabulary Skill 17

Lesson 2:   There Once Was a Cowgirl
               by Margaret Fetty
Teacher Information 18
Poem 19
Assessment 20
Vocabulary Skill 21

Lesson 3:   Have You Ever Seen?
               by Anonymous
Teacher Information 22
Poem 23
Assessment 24
Vocabulary Skill 25

Lesson 4:   Two Little Kittens
               by Anonymous
Teacher Information 26
Poem 27
Assessment 28
Vocabulary Skill 29

**Lesson 5:   [from] How the Camel Got His
               Hump**
               by Rudyard Kipling
Teacher Information 30
Poem 31
Assessment 32
Vocabulary Skill 33

Unit 3: Me, Myself, and I
Lesson 6:   Number Slumber
               by Thomasin Heyworth
Teacher Information 34
Poem 35
Assessment 36
Vocabulary Skill 37

Lesson 7:   Voices
               by Witter Bynner
Teacher Information 38
Poem 39
Assessment 40
Vocabulary Skill 41

Lesson 8:   I Went to Sea
               by Hilda Conkling
Teacher Information 42
Poem 43
Assessment 44
Vocabulary Skill 45

Contents
Poetry: Grade 3, SV 9893-0

Lesson 9:   My Bed Is a Boat
   by Robert Louis Stevenson

Teacher Information 46
Poem 47
Assessment 48
Vocabulary Skill 49

Lesson 10: Afternoon on a Hill
   by Edna St. Vincent Millay

Teacher Information 50
Poem 51
Assessment 52
Vocabulary Skill 53

Unit 4: Nature-ally Fun
Lesson 11: The March Wind
   by Anonymous

Teacher Information 54
Poem 55
Assessment 56
Vocabulary Skill 57

Lesson 12: Dust of Snow
   by Robert Frost

Teacher Information 58
Poem 59
Assessment 60
Vocabulary Skill 61

Lesson 13: Autumn Song
   by Hilda Conkling

Teacher Information 62
Poem 63
Assessment 64
Vocabulary Skill 65

Lesson 14: The Gardener
   by Robert Louis Stevenson

Teacher Information 66
Poem 67
Assessment 68
Vocabulary Skill 69

Lesson 15: Who Has Seen the Wind?
   by Christina Rossetti

Teacher Information 70
Poem 71
Assessment 72
Vocabulary Skill 73

Unit 5: Animal Acts
Lesson 16: The Eagle
   by Alfred, Lord Tennyson

Teacher Information 74
Poem 75
Assessment 76
Vocabulary Skill 77

Lesson 17: A Bird's Home
   by Margaret Fetty

Teacher Information 78
Poem 79
Assessment 80
Vocabulary Skill 81

Lesson 18: To a Butterfly
   by William Wordsworth

Teacher Information 82
Poem 83
Assessment 84
Vocabulary Skill 85

Lesson 19: The Feeder
   by Thomasin Heyworth

Teacher Information 86
Poem 87
Assessment 88
Vocabulary Skill 89

Lesson 20: The Little Mouse
   by Mother Goose

Teacher Information 90
Poem 91
Assessment 92
Vocabulary Skill 93

Answer Key 94

Poetry: Grade 3, SV 9893-0

Grade 3
Poetry Comprehension Skills

Introduction

This book is designed to help students become better readers through the reading of poetry. The IRA/NCTE Standards for the English Language Arts list as the first recommendation: "Students read a wide range of print and nonprint texts to build an understanding of texts, of themselves, and of the cultures of the United States and the world…." Poetry is a form of literature easily read and enjoyed by students of all ages. Children's books often use the rhythm and rhyme of poetry to engage young readers. Poetry helps develop language skills and is often used in phonemic awareness techniques. Moreover, since poetry often uses figurative speech, it encourages imagination and creative thinking. As students progress, their enjoyment of poetry grows to encompass different forms and styles. Most students not only enjoy reading poetry, but they enjoy creating their own verse as well. Finally, most assessment tests now include poetry. These tests include both multiple choice and short-answer questions. It is important that students become comfortable with the format so as to be confident when they encounter it in testing situations.

The Poetry Series

This reproducible poetry series will supplement any reading program. Each lesson tests comprehension skills as well as offers suggestions for vocabulary and fluency development, two essential skills for reading and language development.

Organization of the Poetry Series

The book is divided into four thematic units which will help the teacher integrate poetry into other content areas. The units are On the Silly Side; Me, Myself, and I; Nature-ally Fun; and Animal Acts. There are five poems in each unit. The lesson components are explained below.

Teacher Information

The first page of every lesson provides explicit instructions for teaching the poem. There are specific sections that address multiple skills. To begin, each poem is summarized. A list of words that students may find difficult to read or understand is included as well. Another section lists a specific poetry standard and outlines an activity that will help students explore the concept. A third section outlines how to introduce the poem and the vocabulary words, as well as includes ideas for fluency practice. Finally, a fun and creative writing suggestion helps students think about the topic or a specific skill to extend the lesson.

Poem

The poems were selected to complement topics taught at each grade level. Illustrations on the page support the topic to help students better understand the content.

Assessment

Each poem is followed by a seven-question assessment. The first six questions are in a standardized-test format and focus on six important comprehension skills. They always follow a prescribed order:

1. Facts The first question focuses on literal comprehension. Students identify pieces of factual information. They look for details that tell who, what, when, where, and how.

2. Sequence The second question refers to sequence. Students practice identifying the order of events or the steps in a process.

3. Context In the third question, students are required to practice using all the words in the poem to understand unfamiliar words. Students become aware of the relationships between words, phrases, and sentences.

4. Main Idea In this question, students will identify the overall point made in the poem. Students must be able to differentiate between the main idea and details.

5. Conclusion The fifth question requires students to draw conclusions. Conclusions are not stated in the reading but must be formulated. Students draw conclusions based only on the information in the poem.

6. Inference The sixth question asks students to make inferences by combining their own knowledge and experience with what they read. They put the facts together to make a reasonable inference about something that is not stated in the poem.

7. Short Answer The final question requires that students write a brief response to a higher-level question.

Other Components

• **Standards** A list of grade-level, poetry-specific standards is found on page 5. A chart highlights in which lesson each standard is introduced.

• **Glossary** Poetry terms and definitions for use by the teacher and older students are given on page 6. Some of the elements are not introduced to younger students in this poetry series since they require advanced knowledge.

• **General Assessment** A two-page assessment is found on pages 7 and 8. It can be used as a pretest to gauge students' understanding of the comprehension skills. It can also be used as a posttest to determine improvements after exposure to poetic literature.

• **Graphic Organizers** Five graphic organizers are provided on pages 9–13 to support different activities and skill development suggested in various lessons.

Poetry: Grade 3, SV 9893-0

Poetry Standards • Grade 3

The following standards focus specifically on poetry and are accepted by many states as important to students in the third grade.

Standard	Lesson
Distinguish between fiction, nonfiction, poetry, plays, and narratives	3, 7, 8
Identify a concrete poem	17
Identify a limerick	2
Identify words that develop auditory skills, including alliteration, onomatopoeia, assonance, and consonance	6, 11, 16, 18, 20
Identify rhyme	10, 12, 14
Identify rhythm	4, 9, 19
Recognize the use of repetition	5, 15
Recognize the use of personification	1, 13
Describe characters, setting, and important events in fiction and poetry	All poems
Read stories, poems, and passages with fluency and expression	All poems

Glossary

alliteration the repetition of the same beginning sound, usually a consonant, in a phrase or line of poetry. Tongue twisters use alliteration. Example: *She sells seashells by the seashore.*

analogy a likeness between two things that are not alike in other ways. Example: *the wings of a bird and the arms of a person*

assonance the repetition of similar vowel sounds in words so they are close in sound, but do not rhyme. Example: *She feeds the deer.*

ballad a long poem written about a famous person or event

cinquain a formula poem that has five lines and a total of 22 syllables, distributed in a specific 2–4–6–8–2 pattern

concrete a poem in which the words, letters, or shape of the poem match the topic

consonance the close repetition of identical consonant sounds before and after different vowels. Example: *flip—flop; feel—fill*

diamante a formula poem that is shaped like a diamond, and the words describe opposite ideas

haiku a formula poem that has three lines and a total of 17 syllables, often distributed in a specific 5–7–5 pattern

imagery the author's use of description and words to create pictures in the reader's mind

limerick a humorous formula poem that has five lines, an "aabba" rhyming pattern, and a specific rhythm

metaphor the comparison of two things in which one is said to be another. Metaphors do not use the words *like* or *as*. Example: *The lake was a golden mirror.*

meter the cadence, or beat, of a poem

onomatopoeia a sound device in which a word makes the sound. Examples: *crash, bang*

personification a device in which human qualities and ideas are given to things. Example: *The wind whispered through the trees.*

poetry an expression of ideas or feeling in words. Poetry usually has form, rhythm, and rhyme.

repetition a sound device in which sounds, words, or phrases are repeated to emphasize a point

rhyme two or more lines that end with rhyming words

rhyming words words that end in the same sounds

rhythm the repeated meter, or beat, in a poem

simile the comparison of two things that are not really alike by using the words *like* or *as*. Example: *Her smile was like sunshine.*

sonnet a poem with 14 lines and a specific rhyming and rhythm pattern

stanza a group of related lines in a poem

tanka a formula poem that has five lines and a total of 31 syllables, distributed in a specific 5–7–5–7–7 pattern

Young Night-Thought

by Robert Louis Stevenson

All night long and every night,
When my mama puts out the light,
I see the people marching by,
As plain as day before my eye.

Armies and emperors and kings,
All carrying different kinds of things,
And marching in so grand a way,
You never saw the like by day.

So fine a show was never seen
At the great circus on the green;
For every kind of beast and man
Is marching in that caravan.

At first they move a little slow,
But still the faster on they go,
And still beside me close I keep
Until we reach the town of Sleep.

Go on to the next page.

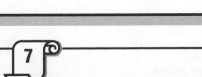

Understand the Poem

Young Night-Thought: Assessment

Think about the poem. Then answer the questions. Fill in the circle next to the correct answer.

1. What marches by in the poem?
   Ⓐ the child's family
   Ⓑ sleepy children
   Ⓒ people and animals

2. At first, the caravan
   Ⓐ moves slowly.
   Ⓑ is hard to see.
   Ⓒ moves by quickly.

3. In the poem, a "beast" is
   Ⓐ a person.
   Ⓑ a monster.
   Ⓒ an animal.

4. This poem is mostly about
   Ⓐ a circus.
   Ⓑ falling asleep.
   Ⓒ traveling.

5. The poem says, "I see the people marching by,/As plain as day before my eye." You can tell that
   Ⓐ the child's room is full of people.
   Ⓑ the people leave before he falls asleep.
   Ⓒ the child is imagining the people.

6. When "we reach the town of Sleep,"
   Ⓐ the child falls asleep.
   Ⓑ the people and animals disappear.
   Ⓒ the child wakes.

7. Why did the poet choose the title "Young Night-Thought" for the poem?

   _____

   _____

Name _____ Date _____

KWL Chart

Topic: _____

K (Know)	W (Want to Know)	L (Learned)

Resources: KWL Chart
Poetry: Grade 3, SV 9893-0

Concept Web

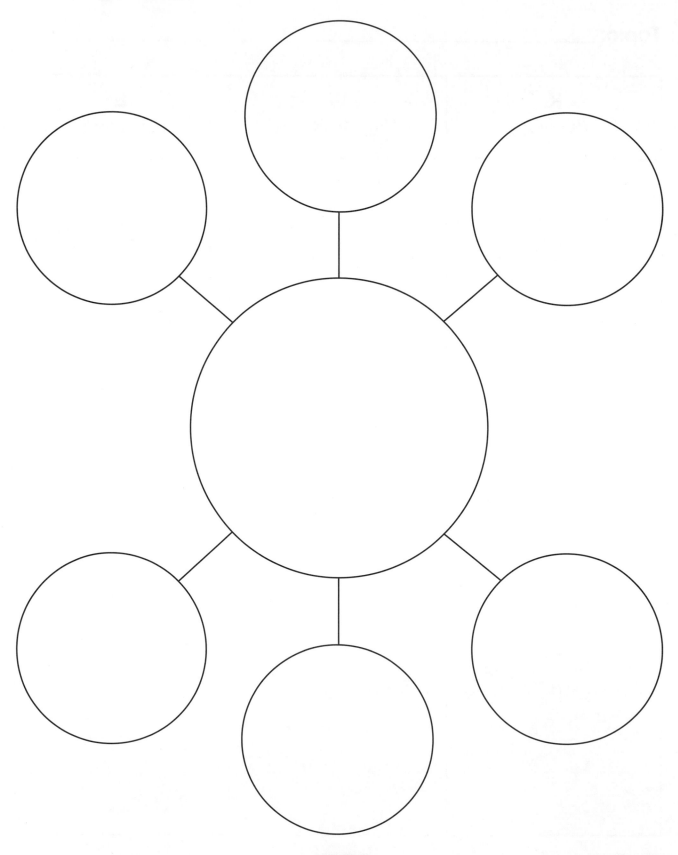

Resources: Concept Web
Poetry: Grade 3, SV 9893-0

Name _____ Date _____

Graph

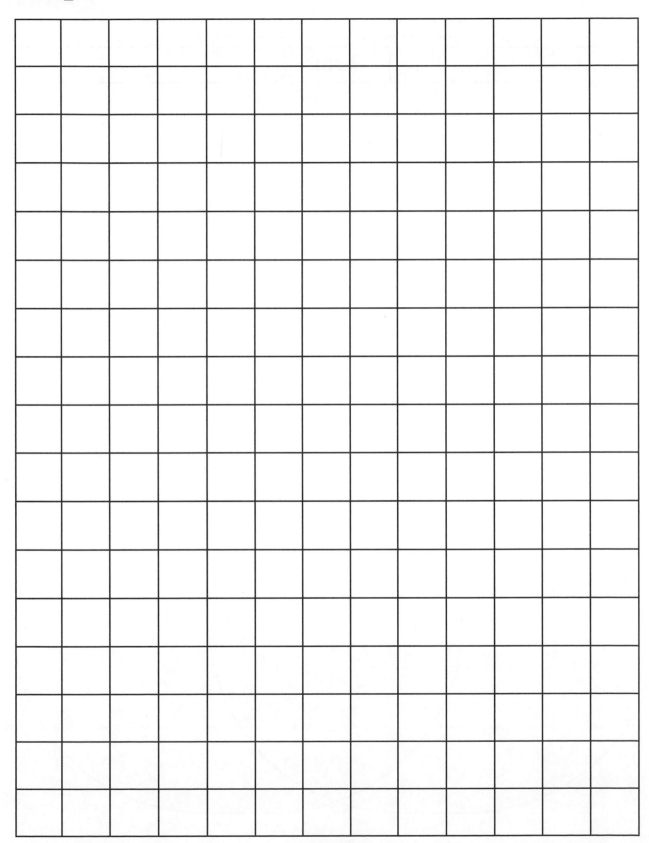

Resources: Graph
Poetry: Grade 3, SV 9893-0

Name _____   Date _____

Venn Diagram

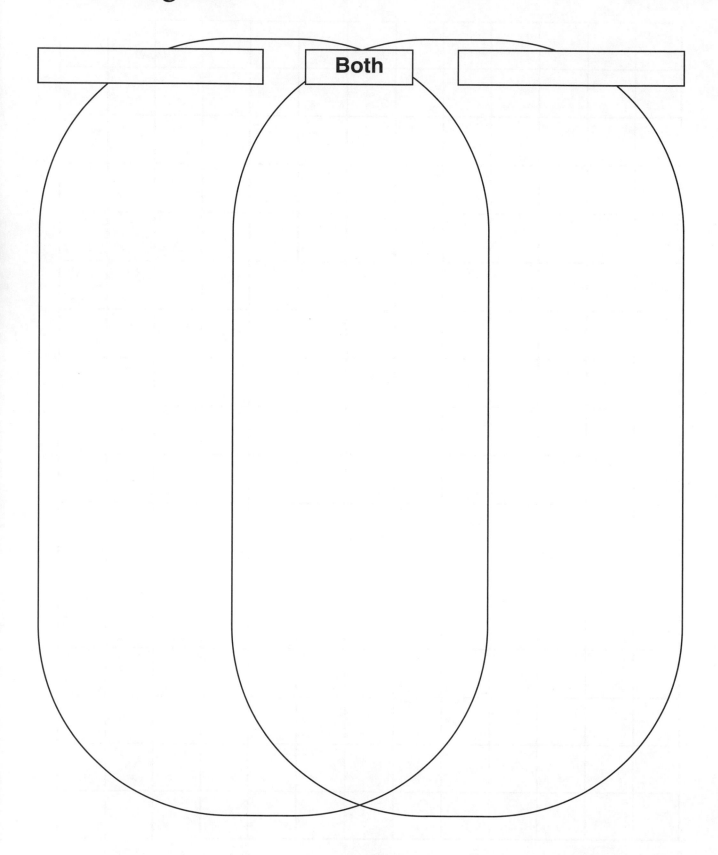

	Both	

Resources: Venn Diagram
Poetry: Grade 3, SV 9893-0

Step Book

Cut out the four pages.
Lay the pages one on top of the other.
Bind the pages at the top.

                                      Poetry: Grade 3, SV 9893-0

April

Poetry Skill: Personification

Standard
Recognize the use of personification

Explore Personification
Explain to students that personification is a device in which human actions and ideas are given to things. Then discuss the examples *the wind whispered through the trees* and *the flames of the fire danced on the wood.*

Vocabulary

clouds–gray or white masses of tiny drops of water floating high in the sky
dears–much loved persons or things
sunbeams–rays of sunlight
tears–drops of salty water that come from the eye

Summary

In this humorous poem, two clouds bump together, causing rain.

Read the Poem

Introduce the Poem
Lead students in a discussion of what causes rain. Then ask them to listen to a poem that has an interesting way to describe a science concept.

Introduce the Vocabulary
Write the vocabulary words on the board. Have partners alphabetize the words, find the definitions in a dictionary, and record the meanings. Challenge students to write sentences with the words.

During Reading

Invite volunteers to read the poem.

After Reading

Questions
1. What causes it to rain in the poem? (*Two clouds bump heads, and they cry.*)
2. What dries the tears? (*the sun's sunbeams*)
3. How are the make-believe events that cause rain like what really happens? (*When clouds bump into each other, they make lightning. Clouds that are full of moisture rain.*)
4. Which words in the poem rhyme? (*sky/cry; dears/tears*)

Fluency
Point out that the quotation marks mean that someone is talking. Then ask how the sun might talk to some clouds. Encourage pairs of students to take turns reading the quotation with expression.

Develop Oral Language
Invite groups of students to act out the poem as they read.

Writing

Review examples of personification in the poem. Then invite students to write and illustrate their own examples of other sky elements, such as the stars or moon, personified.

Name _____   Date _____

April
by Anonymous

Two little clouds one April day
    Went sailing across the sky.
They went so fast that they bumped their heads,
    And both began to cry.

The big round sun came out and said,
    "Oh, never mind, my dears,
I'll send all my sunbeams down
    To dry your fallen tears."

Lesson 1 • April: Poem
Poetry: Grade 3, SV 9893-0

Name _____ Date _____

April: Assessment

Think about the poem. Then answer the questions. Fill in the circle next to the correct answer.

1. What dries the tears?
Ⓐ towels
Ⓑ rainbows
Ⓒ sunbeams

2. What happened before the clouds cried?
Ⓐ They went sailing.
Ⓑ The sunbeams came down.
Ⓒ The sun came out.

3. What is the poet talking about when using the phrase "bumped their heads"?
Ⓐ The clouds moved very fast.
Ⓑ The clouds ran into each other.
Ⓒ The clouds ran into a bump.

4. The poet wrote this poem to
Ⓐ explain why it rains in a fun way.
Ⓑ tell why people need the sun.
Ⓒ explain why people cry.

5. The clouds' tears are really
Ⓐ snow.
Ⓑ ice.
Ⓒ rain.

6. "April" is a good name for this poem because
Ⓐ April is a rainy time of year.
Ⓑ the sun shines a lot in April.
Ⓒ people cry in April.

7. How does the poet feel about rain? How do you know?

_____

_____

Name _____ Date _____

Compound Words

A compound word is a word made by putting together two or more words.

Examples: outside   sidewalk

Draw a line to match one word in Column A with a word in Column B to make a compound word. Use each word only once. Write each new compound word in the box and draw a picture to show its meaning. On another sheet of paper, write a paragraph using at least three of the compound words.

Column A   **Column B**

1. rain   beam   1.

2. over   drops   2.

3. sun   ground   3.

4. thunder   head   4.

5. play   storm   5.

There Once Was a Cowgirl

Poetry Skill: Limerick

Standard
Identify a limerick

Identify a Limerick
Explain that a limerick is a special kind of humorous, five-line poem that has a specific rhythm and rhyming pattern. Read the poem several times and emphasize the rhythm. Then ask questions that guide students to find the "aabba" rhyming pattern.

Vocabulary

cowgirl–a girl who works on a cattle ranch
lariat–a long rope with a loop on one end
practiced–did an action again and again to learn a skill
suddenly–happening quickly
wrapped–covered

Summary

In this limerick, Harriet gets entangled in her lariat when she does a rope trick.

Read the Poem

Introduce the Poem
In advance, make a lariat out of a heavy rope. Then lead students in a discussion to identify the jobs that cowboys and cowgirls do on a ranch. Display the lariat model and invite students to lasso the back of a chair with a lariat.

Introduce the Vocabulary
Write the vocabulary words and the definitions on the board. Lead students in a brief discussion of the words. Then have students create a crossword puzzle with the words using the graph on page 11. Challenge students to write sentences as clues to complete the puzzle.

During Reading

Invite volunteers to read the poem.

After Reading

Questions
1. What was Harriet doing? (*riding a horse and practicing rope tricks*)
2. What might have caused Harriet to put her arm down when the horse stopped? (*Possible answer: She was going to lose her balance and needed the other arm to stay on the horse.*)
3. How do you think Harriet felt at the end of the limerick? (*Possible answers: surprised, frustrated, or embarrassed*)

Fluency
Remind students that a limerick has a specific rhythm. Then model how to read a limerick. Invite partners to practice reading rhythmically.

Develop Oral Language
Invite partners to read the poem according to the rhyming words. One person reads the lines that have the rhyming "a" pattern, and the partner reads the lines with the "b" pattern. Then have partners switch lines.

Writing

Have students imagine themselves as a cowboy or cowgirl. Have them draw a picture of something they would like to do. Then have them write a paragraph or limerick about the job.

Name _____   Date _____

There Once Was a Cowgirl

by Margaret Fetty

There once was a cowgirl named Harriet,
Who practiced rope tricks with a lariat.
When her horse suddenly stopped,
Harriet's arm quickly dropped,
And the lariat wrapped around Harriet.

Understand the Poem

There Once Was a Cowgirl: Assessment

Think about the poem. Then answer the questions. Fill in the circle next to the correct answer.

1. Harriet was a
   Ⓐ horse.
   Ⓑ cowgirl.
   Ⓒ farmer.

2. What happened when the horse stopped?
   Ⓐ The rope dropped.
   Ⓑ The rope wrapped around the horse.
   Ⓒ Harriet's arm dropped.

3. Another name for "lariat" is
   Ⓐ lasso.
   Ⓑ tricks.
   Ⓒ reins.

4. The poem is mostly about
   Ⓐ making rope.
   Ⓑ roping cows.
   Ⓒ a rope trick.

5. Harriet most likely lives
   Ⓐ in a city.
   Ⓑ on a ranch.
   Ⓒ by the lake.

6. Harriet will probably
   Ⓐ practice the rope trick again.
   Ⓑ give up doing rope tricks.
   Ⓒ show her rope trick to a friend.

7. What pattern can you find in a limerick?

_____

_____

Name _____   Date _____

Suffixes

A suffix is a small word part added to the end of a root word that changes the word's meaning.

Root Word	Suffix	Meaning	Example
quiet	est	most	quietest
hope	ful	full of or able to	hopeful
quick	ly	in a certain way	quickly

Read each sentence. Underline each word that has a suffix. Tell the meaning of the word. Use a dictionary if you need to.

1. Leo was happiest when he rode his horse.

Meaning: _____

2. He felt joyful as he galloped around the ranch.

Meaning: _____

3. He rode quickly across the field.

Meaning: _____

4. Suddenly, Leo stopped his horse.

Meaning: _____

5. "How forgetful I am," he said.

Meaning: _____

6. "I need my longest lariat to rope the cows!"

Meaning: _____

Lesson 2 • There Once Was a Cowgirl: Vocabulary Skills
Poetry: Grade 3, SV 9893-0

Have You Ever Seen?

Poetry Skill: Format

Standard
Distinguish between fiction, nonfiction, poetry, and plays

Explore Format
Display a story and lead students in a discussion of the format they see, including paragraph formation and sentence length. Then pass out the poem. Have students compare and contrast the poem and story formats. Point out poem terms, including *lines* and *verses,* as students identify them. Guide students to understand that many poems have short lines, verses, and punctuation at the end of line breaks to signal that the sentence continues on the next line. Also point out that some poems indent on a line that has a line break.

Vocabulary

birch–a kind of tree
dancers–people who dance
needle–a metal tool with a point and a hole that is used for sewing
pair–a group of two
plot–the events in a story
river–a stream of water
soccer–a game in which players kick a ball into a goal
sheet–a covering for a bed that is made of fabric

Summary

This humorous poem challenges the reader to explore the relationships between uncommon items through homographs.

Read the Poem

Introduce the Poem
Write the first line of the poem on the board. Circle *river bed* and ask students how a river bed and a bed they sleep in are alike. Then have them tell which kind of bed a sheet would be used on. Ask students to picture in their mind what a river would look like if it were covered in a sheet. Finally, tell them that the entire poem plays with words and to listen carefully to find the silly pictures.

Introduce the Vocabulary
Write the vocabulary words and the definitions on separate cards. Put them in a pocket chart in any order. Say a sentence with a vocabulary word and ask a volunteer to find the word and its definition in the pocket chart.

During Reading

Invite volunteers to read different verses of the poem.

After Reading

Questions
1. Where is the foot of a mountain? (*at the bottom of the mountain*)
2. What is the foot of the mountain being compared to? (*a person's foot*)
3. Why is this poem funny? (*The poem plays with words that have multiple meanings.*)
4. Which word play do you like the best? (*Answers will vary.*)

Fluency
Remind students that a question mark signals that the sentence is asking something and should be read so that the voice rises at the end. Read the first sentence as a statement and then as a question. Ask students which sounds correct. Then have them practice reading each question to develop fluency.

Develop Oral Language
Have partners alternate reading the rhyming couplets.

Writing

Have students choose a favorite image from the poem. Ask them to draw a picture of the image as described in the poem. For example, students may draw a river covered in a sheet to illustrate the first line of the poem. Have them write the corresponding line from the poem on the paper.

Name _____   Date _____

Have You Ever Seen?
by Anonymous

Have you ever seen a sheet on a river bed?
Or a single hair from a hammer's head?
Has the foot of a mountain any toes?
And is there a pair of garden hose?

Does the needle ever wink its eye?
Why doesn't the wing of a building fly?
Do dancers go to a soccer ball?
Can you open the trunk of a tree at all?

Are the teeth of a rake ever going to bite?
Have the hands of a clock any left or right?
Can the garden plot be deep and dark?
And what is the sound of the birch's bark?

Have You Ever Seen?: Assessment

Think about the poem. Then answer the questions. Fill in the circle next to the correct answer.

1. What might bite in the poem?
- Ⓐ a fork
- Ⓑ a dog
- Ⓒ a rake

2. What does the poet talk about first?
- Ⓐ a river bed
- Ⓑ a soccer ball
- Ⓒ a garden hose

3. A "garden plot" is
- Ⓐ the events in a story.
- Ⓑ a small piece of land.
- Ⓒ a plan.

4. The poem mostly
- Ⓐ plays with words in a fun way.
- Ⓑ tells how people and things are different.
- Ⓒ tells how to do something.

5. The poet writes, "Why doesn't the wing of a building fly?" The poet is comparing the building to
- Ⓐ a hallway.
- Ⓑ a bird.
- Ⓒ kite.

6. The poet probably enjoys
- Ⓐ working in a garden.
- Ⓑ playing soccer.
- Ⓒ telling jokes.

7. What two things are being compared in the question, "Do dancers go to a soccer ball?"

_____

_____

Homographs

Homographs are words that have the same spelling but different meanings. Use words in the sentence to help you choose the correct meaning of a word.

Example: bat
Meaning A: a kind of animal that flies
Meaning B: a kind of toy that hits a ball

Read the questions from the poem "Have You Ever Seen?" Underline each homograph. Then write a sentence using the word in another way.

1. Does the needle ever wink its eye?

_____

2. Why doesn't the wing of a building fly?

_____

3. Can you open the trunk of a tree at all?

_____

4. Are the teeth of a rake ever going to bite?

_____

5. Have the hands of a clock any left or right?

_____

6. And what is the sound of the birch's bark?

_____

Two Little Kittens

Poetry Skill: Rhythm

Standard
Identify rhythm

Explore Rhythm
Explain to students that many poems have a specific rhythm, or beat. Then read the first verse of the poem and clap the beat as you read. Read the entire poem and ask students to clap the beat.

Vocabulary

crept–walked quietly
hiss–the sound an angry cat makes
I'll–I will
stormy–having to do with heavy winds, rain, or snow
swept–moved with a broom
we'll–we will
won't–will not
you'll–you will

Research Base

"All. . .students deserve a deep, rich immersion in poetry as part of their literacy learning." (*Guiding Readers and Writers: Grades 3–6, p. 421*)

Summary

Two kittens fight over a mouse, but they discover the mouse is not important after they spend some time in a winter storm.

Read the Poem

Introduce the Poem

Distribute the KWL chart on page 9 and have students write information that they know about skunks. When they have finished, have students share their responses. Then help students explore why a skunk might need to spray something with its strong scent. Allow them time to write questions about what they would like to know. Then as students read the poem, have them complete the last column in the chart.

Introduce the Vocabulary

Write the vocabulary words and the definitions on separate cards. Pass them out to volunteers. Challenge the students to find the matching word and definition. Then have partners use the word in a sentence.

During Reading

Invite volunteers to read the poem.

After Reading

Questions

1. Who had the mouse? (*the littlest kitten*)
2. How did the kittens end up outside? (*The old woman swept them out with the broom.*)
3. How did the kittens change? (*They went from fighting kittens to very quiet kittens.*)
4. Why did they change? (*The kittens would rather be warm and dry than eat a mouse.*)

Fluency

Direct students to look at the second verse. Point out that the quotation marks are a clue that the characters are speaking. Challenge partners to read the lines as if they were the kittens.

Develop Oral Language

Assign students into groups of three. Have them alternate reading the parts of the poet and the two kittens.

Writing

Have students draw a cartoon strip to show the poem events. Encourage them to include speech bubbles to show what the characters are saying to each other.

Name _____   Date _____

Two Little Kittens
by Anonymous

Two little kittens, one stormy night,
    Began to hiss, and then to fight;
One had a mouse, the other had none,
    And that's the way the fight begun.

"I'll have that mouse," said the biggest cat;
    "You'll have that mouse? We'll see about that!"
"I'll have that mouse," said the oldest son;
    "You won't have the mouse," said the little one.

I told you before it was a stormy night,
    When these two little kittens began to fight;
The old woman grabbed her sweeping broom,
    And swept the two kittens right out of the room.

The ground was covered with ice and snow,
    And the two little kittens had nowhere to go.
So they laid themselves down on the mat at the door,
    While the old woman finished sweeping the floor.

Then they crept in, as quiet as mice,
    All wet with snow, and cold as ice.
For they found it was better, that stormy night,
    To lie down and sleep than to hiss and fight.

Understand the Poem

Two Little Kittens: Assessment

Think about the poem. Then answer the questions. Fill in the circle next to the correct answer.

1. Why were the kittens fighting?
   - Ⓐ They did not want to share the mouse.
   - Ⓑ They did not like each other.
   - Ⓒ One kitten wanted to sleep alone.

2. What happens after the woman sweeps the floor?
   - Ⓐ The kittens fight over the mouse.
   - Ⓑ It begins to storm.
   - Ⓒ The kittens go back into the house.

3. The word "crept" means
   - Ⓐ walked quietly.
   - Ⓑ ran noisily.
   - Ⓒ jumped happily.

4. What lesson did the kittens learn?
   - Ⓐ They should be quiet.
   - Ⓑ They should not fight.
   - Ⓒ They should not eat mice.

5. The old woman sweeps the kittens outside because
   - Ⓐ she does not want them to fight.
   - Ⓑ she is cleaning the house.
   - Ⓒ they do not belong in the house.

6. What most likely happened to the mouse?
   - Ⓐ The biggest cat got it.
   - Ⓑ It ran away when the cats began to fight.
   - Ⓒ The littlest cat got it.

7. What time of year is it? How do you know?

_____

_____

_____

Name _____ Date _____

Contractions

A contraction is a word made from two smaller words. An apostrophe (')
shows that one or more letters are missing in the word.

Examples: you + will = you'll   that + is = that's

✎ **Read each sentence. Look at the
words in dark print. Write the sentence so
that the words are a contraction.**

1. Emile **did not** have a pet.

_____

2. "**I will** ask Dad if I can have a kitten," he said.

_____

3. "**That is** a great idea!" said Mr. Sosa.

_____

4. "But **you will** have to take good care of the kitten," he added.

_____

5. "**Let us** go to the pet shelter now," said Emile.

_____

6. "**We will** find the perfect kitten there!" he exclaimed.

_____

Lesson 4 • Two Little Kittens: Vocabulary Skills
Poetry: Grade 3, SV 9893-0

[from] How the Camel Got His Hump

Poetry Skill: Repetition

Standard
Recognize the use of repetition

Explore Repetition
Repetition is a sound device in which sounds, words, phrases, or sentences are repeated to emphasize a point. As students read the poem, ask them why the poet might repeat the lines: *When we get the hump—/Cameelious hump—/The hump that is black and blue!*

Vocabulary

cure–to make healthy again
frowst–to stand, sit, or lie in a lazy way in a hot, stuffy room
growl–a noise made by a dog that shows anger or fear
grunt–a noise made by a pig
ought–should be
perspire–lightly sweat
scowl–frown
shiver–to shake with cold or fear

Summary

An excerpt from this well-loved poem suggests that grumpy students need to go outside to work to get rid of their "humps."

Read the Poem

Introduce the Poem
Read to students "How the Camel Got His Hump" from Rudyard Kipling's *Just So Stories*. Ask students if they ever feel like the camel. Then ask students to listen to the poem that Rudyard Kipling also wrote.

Introduce the Vocabulary
Write the vocabulary words on the board. Then say a rhyming word for each word and have students find and say the matching rhyming word on the list. Discuss the definitions of each.

During Reading

Invite volunteers to read the poem.

After Reading

Questions
1. According to the poet, why do people get humps? (*They don't have enough to do.*)
2. Why do you think the poet uses the phrase "snarly-yarly voice"? What does he mean? (*Most likely answer: The phrase is fun and gets the reader's attention. He means the person is grumpy and whining.*)
3. Why do you think the poet says that the hump is black and blue? (*Possible answer: They are colors that represent things that are hurt and sad.*)
4. What do you do to get rid of your hump? (*Answers will vary.*)

Fluency
Point out the em-dash in the poem. Explain that an em-dash signals that the reader should briefly pause. Model how to read the refrain and have students rehearse the lines to develop fluency.

Develop Oral Language
Invite students to read the poem chorally.

Writing

Invite students to draw a picture of themselves with a "cameelious" hump! Then have them write a paragraph telling what they do to get rid of their hump.

[from] How the Camel Got His Hump

by Rudyard Kipling

The Camel's hump is an ugly lump
        Which well you may see at the zoo;
But uglier yet is the hump we get
        From having too little to do.

Kiddies and grown-ups too-oo-oo,
If we haven't enough to do-oo-oo,
        We get the hump—
        Cameelious hump—
The hump that is black and blue!

We climb out of bed with a frouzly head,
        And a snarly-yarly voice.
We shiver and scowl and we grunt and we growl
        At our bath and our boots and our toys;

And there ought to be a corner for me
(And I know there is one for you)
        When we get the hump—
        Cameelious hump—
The hump that is black and blue!

The cure for this ill is not to sit still,
        Or frowst with a book by the fire;
But to take a large hoe and a shovel also,
        And dig till you gently perspire.

Name _____ Date _____

[from] How the Camel Got His Hump: Assessment

Think about the poem. Then answer the questions. Fill in the circle next to the correct answer.

1. According to the poem, who can get the hump?
   Ⓐ children only
   Ⓑ children and adults
   Ⓒ camels

2. What happens after people wake up with the hump?
   Ⓐ They are in a bad mood.
   Ⓑ They go to the zoo.
   Ⓒ They read by the fire.

3. The word "frowst" probably means
   Ⓐ play.
   Ⓑ float.
   Ⓒ relax.

4. The poem is telling people
   Ⓐ to stay busy.
   Ⓑ to read more.
   Ⓒ to be like a camel.

5. The hump comes from
   Ⓐ being a camel.
   Ⓑ being lazy.
   Ⓒ digging in the garden.

6. This poet seems to enjoy
   Ⓐ riding camels.
   Ⓑ reading by a fire.
   Ⓒ writing fun poems.

7. Why do you think the poet says that the hump people get is ugly?

_____

_____

Name _____   Date _____

Synonyms

A synonym is a word that means the same or almost the same as another word.

Examples: small—little   happy—glad

 Read each sentence. Find a word in the box that means the same or almost the same as the word in dark print. Write the word on the line.

gently	kiddies	large	perspire	scowl	shiver

1. Mrs. Edwards picked up the **big** shovel.

   _____

2. She began to **frown** as she dug in the dirt.

   _____

3. The cold wind made Mrs. Edwards **shake**.

   _____

4. However, the digging soon made her **sweat**.

   _____

5. She **tenderly** pushed the dirt away from a growing bud.

   _____

6. By the time the **children** ran into the garden, Mrs. Edwards was smiling.

   _____

Number Slumber

Poetry Skill: Alliteration

Standard
Identify words that develop auditory skills, including alliteration, onomatopoeia, assonance, and consonance

Explore Alliteration
Explain that alliteration is a sound device in which the beginning sound or sounds in a group of words are repeated. Have students tell what sound is repeated in *several snakes slither.* Challenge them to find other examples of alliteration.

Vocabulary

anxious–worried
fleets–groups of boats, cars, or airplanes
message–information sent to a person
oodles–lots
relief–a feeling of not having to worry or be in pain
sloops–sailing ships
track–to count
vats–large containers for liquids

Summary

A dreamer is overcome with the number of things that she must count in this humorous poem. But she is even more anxious when she remembers that she has to take a math test that day.

Read the Poem

Introduce the Poem
Invite students to describe some interesting dreams they have had. Then ask them to listen to a poem that describes a dream one poet had.

Introduce the Vocabulary
Write a sentence using each vocabulary word. Challenge students to define the word by using context clues.

During Reading

Invite volunteers to read the poem.

After Reading

Questions
1. Why does the poet call this poem "Number Slumber"? (Slumber *is another word for* sleep. *The poet dreams about numbers while she sleeps.*)
2. What kinds of things does the poet see? (*Answers will vary but should include something from the poem.*)
3. How does this poem make you feel? (*Answers will vary.*)

Fluency
Point out the many different punctuation marks in the final verse. Explain how to pause at commas and show excitement when reading a sentence that ends with an exclamation point. Then model how to read the verse rhythmically and fluently. Challenge students to practice reading the verse.

Develop Oral Language
Point out that this poem has an "abcb" rhyming pattern but that each verse is actually a couplet. Working in pairs, have one student read the first two lines in the couplet, while the partner reads the second two lines.

Writing

Invite students to choose a number and write alliterative sentences with it, such as *ten tons of tuna tap-dancing.* Challenge them to see how many words they can use with the same beginning sound. Then have them draw a picture to illustrate their sentence.

Name _____   Date _____

Number Slumber
by Thomasin Heyworth

Last night I dreamed
Things were never just one,
But numbers of things,
For a while, it was fun!

There were oodles of poodles
And vats of cats,
Groups of sloops—
And much more than that!

I saw several snakes
Slither out through a door,
And when I went, too,
I found dozens more!

There were messes of dresses
And gobs of knobs.
There were fleets of treats.
There was paint by globs!

I saw hundreds of hippos
And trucks of ducks,
Zillions of zebras
And billions of bucks!

A gazillion gorillas
Had tons of toys,
Enough for a million
Girls and boys!

Enter the elephants,
And there were so many,
That I'd have been rich
If for each I'd a penny!

But a message came
To my brain as I slept.
The words, "You must
    count these,"
Into my ear crept.

So I tried and I tried
To count them and yet,
I began to get anxious,
Break into a sweat!

Knee deep in sheep,
I tried to keep track
Of bunches of birds,
And yak upon yak!

I woke with a start,
A relief, I must say!
'Til I remembered the
    math test
That I have today.

Lesson 6 • Number Slumber: Poem
Poetry: Grade 3, SV 9893-0

Understand the Poem

Number Slumber: Assessment

Think about the poem. Then answer the questions. Fill in the circle next to the correct answer.

1. What message came to the poet in the dream?
- (A) Name everything.
- (B) Count everything.
- (C) Take everything home.

2. The dream was fun
- (A) after the dreamer began counting.
- (B) before the dreamer fell asleep.
- (C) when it began.

3. The dreamer thought it was a relief to wake up. Waking up made the dreamer
- (A) angry.
- (B) happy.
- (C) afraid.

4. This poem is mostly about
- (A) colors.
- (B) animals.
- (C) numbers.

5. The dream was about counting because
- (A) the dreamer was thinking about a math test.
- (B) the dreamer likes to count things.
- (C) the dreamer does not know how to count.

6. The dreamer probably
- (A) wants a new bed.
- (B) is afraid of snakes.
- (C) is worried about the math test.

7. Why do you think that the poet was getting anxious near the end of the poem?

_____

_____

Explore More

Dictionary Skills

A dictionary tells how to say a word and what it means.

Look at the pronunciation key. Then circle the word that matches the pronunciation.

a	add	i	it	o͝o	took	oi	oil
ā	ace	ī	ice	o͞o	pool	ou	pout
â	care	o	odd	u	up	ng	ring
ä	palm	ō	open	û	burn	th	thin
e	end	ô	order	yo͞o	fuse	th	this
ē	equal					zh	vision

ə = { a in *above*   e in *sicken*   i in *possible*
      o in *melon*   u in *circus* }

1. (vats)
vase   vats   vast

2. (slo͞ops)
slops   slopes   sloops

3. (flēts)
fleets   felts   feels

4. (trak)
train   track   trial

5. (o͞od´ lz)
odds   only   oodles

6. (mes´ əj)
message   magic   messy

7. (ank´ shəs)
ankles   anxious   action

8. (ri lēf´)
rifle   reef   relief

Voices

Poetry Skill: Format

Standard
Distinguish between fiction, nonfiction, poetry, and plays

Explore Format
Display a story and lead students in a discussion of the format they see, including paragraph formation and sentence length. Then pass out the poem. Have students compare and contrast the poem and story formats on the Venn diagram found on page 12.

Summary

The poet talks about a person he remembers at a party.

Read the Poem

Introduce the Poem
Pass out the concept web found on page 10. Ask students to write words and phrases that describe parties they go to. Then invite them to share special party memories. Explain that they will listen to a poem that tells about a party the poet attended.

Introduce the Vocabulary
Write the words on index cards, making several sets. Pass the cards out so that each student has one. Have them look in the dictionary to find the meaning of the word on the card. Then have students with the same card form a group. Challenge them to write a sentence with the word. Ask each group to share the sentences.

During Reading

Read the poem to students.

After Reading

Questions
1. What kind of party did the poet go to? (*It was a big party with lots of people and food.*)
2. What does the phrase "there were many voices vying" mean? (*Everyone was talking at the same time.*)
3. Why would the poet remember someone who did not talk much? (*Answers will vary.*)
4. Do you think the poet liked the party? (*Most likely answer: No, because he remembered the quietest person there.*)

Vocabulary

feast–a big meal
least–the smallest part
motions–moves
to and fro–back and forth
voices–the sound made when people talk, sing, or yell
vying–trying

Fluency
Help students explore how to read poems with line breaks. Model how to read the poem rhythmically and without pause at the end of an unpunctuated line. Then have partners rehearse the poem several times.

Develop Oral Language
Invite students to alternate reading the lines of the poem.

Writing

Invite students to write their own poem about a party. Suggest they use the concept web completed in Introduce the Poem.

Research Base

"Students who are immersed in the vibrant sounds of poetry will write better poetry themselves; what's more, they are more likely to develop a lifetime appreciation for poetry."
(*Guiding Readers and Writers: Grades 3–6, p. 419*)

Voices

by Witter Bynner

O, there were lights and laughter
    And the motions to and fro
Of people as they enter
    And people as they go…
And there were many voices
    Vying at the feast,
But mostly I remember
    Yours—who spoke the least.

Name _____   Date _____

Voices: Assessment

Think about the poem. Then answer the questions.
Fill in the circle next to the correct answer.

1. What did some of the voices in the poem do?
  Ⓐ yell
  Ⓑ laugh
  Ⓒ whisper

2. When did the poet write the poem?
  Ⓐ before the party
  Ⓑ during the party
  Ⓒ after the party

3. What does "motions" mean?
  Ⓐ moving about
  Ⓑ feeling happy or sad
  Ⓒ laughing loudly

4. The poet wrote the poem
  Ⓐ to teach readers about different kinds of voices.
  Ⓑ to describe a person he remembered.
  Ⓒ to tell readers an exciting story about a party.

5. How do you know that the poem takes place at a party?
  Ⓐ There were lights, laughter, and a feast.
  Ⓑ People were leaving.
  Ⓒ There was lots of noise.

6. The poet probably likes to
  Ⓐ play games.
  Ⓑ eat food.
  Ⓒ watch people.

7. Do you think that the person the poet remembers liked the party? Why or why not?

_____

_____

Name _____ Date _____

Words in Context

Use other words in sentences to help you find the missing word.

Read each sentence. Find a word or words from the box to complete it. Then write the word or words on the line.

feast	to and fro	least	motions	voices	vying

1. The students ran _____ in the backyard.

2. Their _____ rose in laughter as they sprayed each other with water.

3. They were _____ to see who would stay dry the longest.

4. The smallest student, who had moved the _____, was soaked.

5. The table was filled with food, and the _____ was ready to begin.

6. Mrs. West made _____ with her hands to call the guests to the table.

LESSON 8

I Went to Sea

Poetry Skill: Format

Standard
Distinguish between fiction, nonfiction, poetry, and plays

Explore Format
Remind students that a poem can be a short and quick picture of a feeling or thought a poet wants to share. Then lead students in a discussion of how the structure of "I Went to Sea" shows that it is a poem. Guide the discussion so that students understand that not all poems rhyme.

Vocabulary

loveliest–most lovely
valleys–the low land between mountains and hills
jewels–gems
wandering–moving without direction
secrets–things few people know about
dangling–hanging
creature–animal

Teacher Tips

You may want to gather pictures of the sea life mentioned in the poem.

Summary

A poet tells of the amazing sea life she sees when she takes a trip in a glass-bottomed boat.

Read the Poem

Distribute the KWL chart on page 9 and have students write information that they know about sea life. When completed, have students share their responses. Allow them time to write questions about what they would like to know. Then as students read the poem, have them complete the last column in the chart.

Introduce the Vocabulary

Write the vocabulary words and the definitions on separate cards. Put them in a pocket chart in any order. Say a sentence with a vocabulary word and ask a volunteer to find the word and the definition that matches.

During Reading

Read the poem to students.

After Reading

Questions

1. What is a glass-bottomed boat? (*a boat that has a clear bottom so people can see things in the water as the boat moves*)
2. Who are the "children of the sea"? (*the fish*)
3. How does the poet feel about the sea? How do you know? (*She likes the sea because she describes it in an interesting, fun way.*)
4. How is this poem different from other poems we have read? (*Possible answer: It does not rhyme or have rhythm.*)

Fluency

Write ellipsis points on the board and explain that they are a kind of punctuation. Tell students that a writer will use ellipsis points to show that the thought continues after a brief pause. Model how to read a sentence from the poem with ellipsis points. Challenge students to practice reading the same sentence.

Develop Oral Language

Challenge students to retell the poem in their own words.

Writing

Remind students that the poem does not use rhyming words. However, the poet does use describing words to help the reader see what she is thinking. Then ask students to imagine that they have traveled to a new place. Invite them to write a poem describing what they saw.

Name _____ Date _____

I Went to Sea

by Hilda Conkling

I went to sea in a glass-bottomed boat
And found that the loveliest shells of all
Are hidden below in valleys of sand.
I saw coral and sponge and weed
And bubbles like jewels dangling.
I saw a creature with eyes of mist
Go by slowly.
Starfish fingers held the water . . .
Let it go again . . .
I saw little fish, the children of the sea;
They were gay and busy.
I wanted the seaweed purple; I wanted the shells;
I wanted a little fish to hold in my hands;
I wanted the big fish to stop wandering about,
And tell me all they knew . . .
I have come back safe and dry
And know no more secrets
Than yesterday!

I Went to Sea: Assessment

➤ **Think about the poem. Then answer the questions. Fill in the circle next to the correct answer.**

1. Where does the poet think the loveliest shells are?

Ⓐ on the beach

Ⓑ in her boat

Ⓒ under the sea

2. The poet finds that she is "safe and dry"

Ⓐ after she comes back.

Ⓑ while she is in the boat.

Ⓒ before she goes in the boat.

3. A creature has "eyes of mist." This probably means its eyes are

Ⓐ bright.

Ⓑ colorful.

Ⓒ not clear.

4. This poem is mostly about

Ⓐ a starfish.

Ⓑ the wonders of the sea.

Ⓒ how to sail a boat.

5. The bubbles most likely make the poet think of jewels because

Ⓐ the bubbles sparkle like jewels.

Ⓑ the bubbles are expensive like jewels.

Ⓒ the bubbles are on a necklace.

6. The poet learns no secrets because

Ⓐ she did not ask the right questions.

Ⓑ the fish cannot talk.

Ⓒ she did not go swimming.

7. How do you know that "I Went to Sea" is a poem?

_____

_____

www.harcourtschoolsupply.com

44

Lesson 8 • I Went to Sea: Poem Assessment
Poetry: Grade 3, SV 9893-0

Classify

Explore More

Think about how words and things you read are alike. It can help you better understand what you are reading.

Read each group of words. Cross out the word that does not belong.

1. hanging   ring   dangling   swinging

2. cookies   jewels   gems   stones

3. valleys   mountains   cars   hills

4. beautiful   lovely   pretty   circle

5. wall   beast   creature   animal

6. whispers   sea   secrets   hidden

LESSON 9

My Bed Is a Boat

Summary

The poet compares his bed to a boat when he sleeps.

Read the Poem

Introduce the Poem
Lead students in a discussion of bedtime preparations. Have volunteers share special things they do. Have students list common bedtime preparations, such as brushing teeth and saying good-night. Then tell students that they are going to read a poem about one boy's thoughts about bedtime.

Introduce the Vocabulary
Write several sets of vocabulary words on index cards. Pass them out so that each student has one. Write each word on the board one at a time and say the word. Give the definition. Ask students holding that card to form a group. After all words have been named, ask each group to write a sentence using the word.

During Reading

Read the poem aloud to students.

After Reading

Questions
1. What does the poet compare sleeping to? (*taking a trip on a boat*)
2. What do you think is the poet's "sailor's coat"? (*his pajamas*)
3. What does the poet mean when he says, "I shut my eyes and sail away"? (*He goes to sleep.*)
4. What patterns do you notice in this poem? (*There is a rhyming "abab" pattern and a meter pattern.*)

Fluency
Explain that many poems have a rhythm, or beat. Model how to read the poem rhythmically. Then invite partners to practice reading the poem with the same rhythm and speed.

Develop Oral Language
Invite partners to alternate reading couplets.

Writing

Remind students that the poet compares his bed and sleeping to a boat and sailing trip. Have them complete a concept web on page 9 to list actions and equipment needed to do a hobby or a favorite sport. Then have them think about how the hobby or sport is like something they do at home or school. Challenge students to write a paragraph or poem telling how the two are alike.

My Bed Is a Boat
by Robert Louis Stevenson

My bed is like a little boat;
    Nurse helps me in when I embark;
She girds me in my sailor's coat
    And starts me in the dark.

At night I go on board and say
    Good-night to all my friends on shore;
I shut my eyes and sail away
    And see and hear no more.

And sometimes things to bed I take,
    As prudent sailors have to do;
Perhaps a slice of wedding-cake,
    Perhaps a toy or two.

All night across the dark we steer;
    But when the day returns at last,
Safe in my room beside the pier,
    I find my vessel fast.

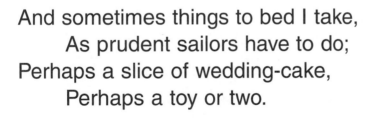

Understand the Poem

My Bed Is a Boat: Assessment

Think about the poem. Then answer the questions. Fill in the circle next to the correct answer.

1. The poet compares the child's bed to
   Ⓐ a nurse.
   Ⓑ a sailor.
   Ⓒ a boat.

2. After sailing all night,
   Ⓐ the child gets into his bed.
   Ⓑ the child wakes.
   Ⓒ the child eats a piece of cake.

3. The poem says, "Nurse helps me in when I embark." "Embark" probably means
   Ⓐ leave.
   Ⓑ complain.
   Ⓒ swim.

4. The poet probably wrote this poem to
   Ⓐ tell how to sail a bed.
   Ⓑ compare sleeping to sailing away.
   Ⓒ explain what the child's nurse does.

5. The child's nurse is probably
   Ⓐ another child.
   Ⓑ his mother.
   Ⓒ someone who takes care of him.

6. The child in the poem
   Ⓐ has a good imagination.
   Ⓑ does not like to sleep.
   Ⓒ has never been on a boat.

7. What are some ways that the poet compares sleeping to sailing?

_____

_____

Name _____   Date _____

Troublesome Words

Some words sound alike, but they have different spellings and meanings.

Example: I **ate** breakfast at **eight** o'clock.

ate = chewed and swallowed food

eight = the number 8

Read each sentence. Circle the words that sound alike. Then find the words in a dictionary. Write the meaning of each word.

1. Tony went to see the sea.

_____

_____

2. There were tickets on sale to go for a sail on a boat.

_____

_____

3. There were two tickets left to buy.

_____

_____

4. Tony was bored until he got to board a boat.

_____

_____

Lesson 9 • **My Bed Is a Boat:** Vocabulary Skills
Poetry: Grade 3, SV 9893-0

Afternoon on a Hill

Poetry Skill: Rhyming Words

Standard
Identify rhyme

Explore Rhyming Words
Remind students that some poems use rhyming words. Then have students find the rhyming word pairs and circle them using matching crayon colors. Guide them to understand that the even-numbered lines rhyme. Then ask students to choose one of the word pairs. Have them make a step book found on page 13. Challenge students to write and illustrate four new words that rhyme with the pair they chose.

Vocabulary

bow–to bend forward
cliffs–high walls of rock
gladdest–the most glad
mark–to be a sign of
watch–to look
wind–moving air

Summary

The poet spends an afternoon enjoying nature's gifts of beauty.

Read the Poem

Introduce the Poem
Ask students to draw the most beautiful nature scene they have visited. Invite them to share their pictures and how they felt when visiting the place. Then invite students to listen to a poet describe a place that she likes to visit.

Introduce the Vocabulary
Write the vocabulary words on the board and ask volunteers to look up the words in a dictionary. Have the volunteer read all the definitions. Explain to students that some words have multiple meanings. Then have students read the poem to discover which meaning the words have in it.

During Reading

Ask a volunteer to read the poem.

After Reading

Questions
1. Where is the poet? (*somewhere in a field next to a cliff where there are flowers*)
2. How does the poet feel in this poem? (*glad*)
3. Do you think the poet lives in a big or little town? How do you know? (*She lives in a little town because she can pick out the house that is hers.*)
4. What does the poet mean when she says that she looks "with quiet eyes"? (*Possible answer: She doesn't talk or move. She just sits and watches nature.*)

Fluency
Explain that expression is the way a poem is read. Then lead students in a discussion of the mood of the poem. Ask if the poet is excited or calm, happy or sad. Then read the poem several ways: fast and excited, slow and melancholy, and calm and happy. Have students tell which speed and voice reflects the mood of the poem. Point out how the words and images dictate the mood. Finally, have students practice reading the poem expressively.

Develop Oral Language
Have students work in pairs. Have one partner read the first and second lines in each verse and the other student read the third and fourth lines. Ask them to exchange lines on a second reading.

Writing

Invite students to write a poem about the picture they drew during the introduction. Challenge them to use words and images to capture the mood they felt when they visited the place.

Afternoon on a Hill

by Edna St. Vincent Millay

I WILL be the gladdest thing
      Under the sun!
I will touch a hundred flowers
      And not pick one.

I will look at the cliffs and clouds
      With quiet eyes,
Watch the wind bow down the grass,
      And the grass rise.

And when lights begin to show
      Up from the town,
I will mark which must be mine,
      And then start down.

Afternoon on a Hill: Assessment

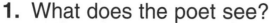 **Think about the poem. Then answer the questions. Fill in the circle next to the correct answer.**

1. What does the poet see?
- Ⓐ birds
- Ⓑ cliffs
- Ⓒ the moon

2. When does the poet go home?
- Ⓐ when the sun rises
- Ⓑ after the sun sets
- Ⓒ before noon

3. Another way to say "watch the wind bow down the grass" is look
- Ⓐ for an arrow in the grass.
- Ⓑ at the wind blow.
- Ⓒ at a dance.

4. Another good title for this poem would be
- Ⓐ "A Hundred Flowers."
- Ⓑ "A Windy Visit."
- Ⓒ "Walking in Nature."

5. The poet is
- Ⓐ with a group of friends.
- Ⓑ with her dog.
- Ⓒ by herself.

6. From the poem, you can tell that the poet
- Ⓐ likes flowers.
- Ⓑ likes to paint.
- Ⓒ likes to climb rock walls.

7. Which senses does the poet use in the poem?

_____

_____

Name _____   Date _____

Homographs

Homographs are words that have the same spelling but different meanings. Sometimes they may have different pronunciations. Use words in the sentence to help you choose the correct meaning of a word.

Example: blue   Meaning A: a color
Meaning B: feeling sad

🪶 **Read each sentence. What does the word in dark print mean? Write the letter for the meaning of the word.**

watch
Meaning A: to look at
Meaning B: a tool that tells time

_____ **1.** Dan's **watch** showed the time to be three o'clock.

_____ **2.** Mrs. Wong likes to **watch** the birds at the park.

wind
Meaning A: moving air
Meaning B: to turn

_____ **3.** Anna will **wind** the key to make the toy move.

_____ **4.** The **wind** blew the leaves off the tree.

bow
Meaning A: to bend forward
Meaning B: a tool that shoots arrows

_____ **5.** People used a **bow** and arrow to hunt long ago.

_____ **6.** Actors come on stage and **bow** after the show.

The March Wind

**Poetry Skill:
Onomatopoeia**

Standard
Identify words that develop auditory skills, including alliteration, onomatopoeia, assonance, and consonance

Explore Onomatopoeia
Onomatopoeia is a sound device often used in poetry to dramatize an event. Introduce the concept by discussing things in nature that make sounds, such as rain and flying bees. Then challenge students to draw a picture of something in nature that makes a sound and have them write the sound word as the label.

Vocabulary

flocks–groups
strew–to spread around
toss–to throw
twigs–thin tree branches
whirl–to spin
whistle–a clear, sharp sound

Summary

Using the voice of the wind, the poet describes what the wind does in March.

Read the Poem

Introduce the Poem
Distribute the KWL chart on page 9 and have students write facts they know about the wind. When they are finished, have students share their responses. Allow them time to write questions they have about the wind. Then, as students read the poem, have them complete the last column in the chart.

Introduce the Vocabulary
Divide the class into small groups and assign each group a vocabulary word. Then distribute the concept web on page 10. Challenge each group to create a web with their word that links it to other images they know.

During Reading

Ask a volunteer to read the poem.

After Reading

Questions
1. Who is speaking in the poem? (*the wind*)
2. The wind says that it comes to work and play. Which actions do you think show that the wind is playing? (*toss the branches, whirl the leaves, strew the twigs, blow the students round*)
3. What picture do you get in your mind when you hear the line, "The frozen earth I sweep"? (*The wind is a giant broom that sweeps the ground.*)

Fluency
Write a semicolon on the board. Explain that this punctuation signals that a reader should briefly pause, just like when reading a period. Model reading the first verse. Then have partners take turns practicing reading semicolons in the first verse.

Develop Oral Language
Have partners choral read the poem.

Writing

Have students choose a favorite activity. Challenge them to list four onomatopoetic words that could be associated with the activity. Ask them to use each word in a sentence that describes the event.

Name _____   Date _____

The March Wind
by Anonymous

I come to work as well as play;
    I'll tell you what I do;
I whistle all the live-long day,
    "Woo-oo-oo-oo! Woo-oo!"

I toss the branches up and down
    And shake them to and fro,
I whirl the leaves in flocks of brown,
    And send them high and low.

I strew the twigs upon the ground,
    The frozen earth I sweep;
I blow the students round and round
    And wake the flowers from sleep.

Name _____ Date _____

The March Wind: Assessment

Think about the poem. Then answer the questions. Fill in the circle next to the correct answer.

1. What sound does the wind make when it blows in the poem?
ⓐ Shhh!
ⓑ Woo-oo!
ⓒ Whoosh!

2. What happens before the wind sends the leaves high and low?
ⓐ It whirls them in the air.
ⓑ It blows them around.
ⓒ It whistles through them.

3. What does the word "strew" mean?
ⓐ to grow
ⓑ to spread around
ⓒ to spin

4. The poem is mostly about
ⓐ the actions of the wind.
ⓑ the spring season.
ⓒ games students play.

5. Which line from the poem helps you know that it is March?
ⓐ "I whistle all the live long day"
ⓑ "I whirl the leaves in flocks of brown"
ⓒ "And wake the flowers from sleep"

6. Who is speaking in this poem?
ⓐ some students
ⓑ the wind
ⓒ a tree

7. How do you think the wind wakes the flowers?

_____

_____

Name _____   Date _____

Sound Words

Some words sound like noises different things make. For example, the wind can make a "woo-oo" or a "whoosh."

 Underline the sound word in each sentence.

1. Pam and her brother heard the thunder rumble in the distance.

2. They needed to find safety before the crash of the lightning.

3. The drip drop of the rain told them that the storm was close.

4. They heard the bark of a dog close by.

5. Then they heard the slam of a door.

6. Their shoes crunched the leaves on the trail as they ran toward the house.

7. Pam began to knock on the door.

8. BOOM! The storm had arrived, but Pam and her brother were safe.

Lesson 11 • **The March Wind:** Vocabulary Skills
Poetry: Grade 3, SV 9893-0

Dust of Snow

**Poetry Skill:
Rhyming Words**

Standard
Identify rhyme

Explore Rhyming Words
The use of rhyming couplets will help students develop an understanding of rhyming words. Have students find the rhyming word pairs and circle them using matching crayon colors. Then have students choose one of the word pairs and brainstorm other words that rhyme with that pair.

Vocabulary

crow–a black bird
dust–tiny pieces of dirt or other material
heart–a part of the body that pumps blood
hemlock–a kind of tree that stays green all winter
mood–the way a person feels
rued–was sorry about

Research Base

"**Poetry** is an essential, integral part of the language/literacy curriculum. . . ." (*Guiding Readers and Writers: Grades 3–6, p. 414*)

Summary

A poet feels much happier after a crow causes snow to fall on him.

Read the Poem

Introduce the Poem

Invite students to share times they were in a bad mood. Ask them what happened to change the bad mood. Then tell students that they will read a poem that tells how one poet was able to change his mood.

Introduce the Vocabulary

Write the vocabulary words and the definitions on the board. Lead students in a brief discussion of the words. Have them identify the pair of words that rhyme. Then have them create a crossword puzzle with the words using the graph on page 11. Challenge students to write sentences as clues to complete the puzzle.

During Reading

Read the poem aloud to students.

After Reading

Questions

1. In what season does the poem take place? How do you know? (*It is winter because there is snow on the tree.*)
2. How did the poet feel before his walk? (*unhappy*)
3. How did he feel at the end of the walk? (*happy*)
4. How would you feel if a bird caused snow to fall on you? (*Answers will vary.*)

Fluency

Explain that many poems have a rhythm, or beat. Model how to read the poem rhythmically. Then invite partners to practice reading the poem with the same rhythm and speed.

Develop Oral Language

Invite students to retell the poem in their own words.

Writing

Remind students that the poem uses rhyming words. Then have them review the list they completed in Explore Rhyming Words above. Challenge them to write a short poem using some of the words.

Name _____   Date _____

Dust of Snow
by Robert Frost

The way a crow
Shook down on me
The dust of snow
From a hemlock tree

Has given my heart
A change of mood
And saved some part
Of a day I had rued.

Dust of Snow: Assessment

**Think about the poem. Then answer the questions.
Fill in the circle next to the correct answer.**

1. What came out of the tree?
   - Ⓐ a crow
   - Ⓑ some snow
   - Ⓒ hemlock

2. The poet felt unhappy
   - Ⓐ after the snow fell on him.
   - Ⓑ after he saw the crow.
   - Ⓒ before the snow fell on him.

3. A "dust of snow" would probably be
   - Ⓐ a lot of snow.
   - Ⓑ a flake of snow.
   - Ⓒ a light snow.

4. This poem is mostly about
   - Ⓐ the crow.
   - Ⓑ the hemlock.
   - Ⓒ the poet's mood.

5. The rest of the poet's day was most likely
   - Ⓐ worse than the beginning.
   - Ⓑ the same as the beginning.
   - Ⓒ better than the beginning.

6. The poet must have found what the crow did to be
   - Ⓐ amusing.
   - Ⓑ frightening.
   - Ⓒ boring.

7. Why do you think the poet is happier after he is covered in snow?

_____

_____

Name _____   Date _____

Hink Pinks

Hink pinks are two words beside each other that rhyme. You can use hink pinks to solve riddles.

Example:
Riddle: What do you call a wind that makes **snow** move?
Hink pink answer: A snow blow

Read each riddle. Answer it with a hink pink. (Hint: Think about the words in dark print.)

1. What do you call a tiny, fine piece of **rust**?

   __r__ __u__ __s__ __t__   ____ ____ ____ ____

2. What do you call **food** that makes you feel better once it is eaten?

   ____ ____ ____ ____   __f__ __o__ __o__ __d__

3. What do you call a small pie shaped like a **heart**?

   A __h__ __e__ __a__ __r__ __t__   ____ ____ ____ ____

4. What kind of **crow** is always late?

   A ____ ____ ____ ____   __c__ __r__ __o__ __w__

Autumn Song

Poetry Skill:
Personification

Standard
Recognize the use of
personification

Explore Personification
Explain to students that
personification is a device
in which human actions
and ideas are given to
things. Then discuss the
examples *the wind
whispered through the
trees* and *the flames of the
fire danced on the wood.*

Vocabulary

autumn–the fall season
bare–not covered
blew–sent a strong current
of air
caterpillars–worm-like
animals that become
butterflies
fairy–small, imaginary
magical being that flies
fluttered–moved with quick
flapping movements
forgotten–did not
remember
sandals–shoes made with
thin straps

Summary

The poet uses personification to describe familiar fall images and events.

Read the Poem

Introduce the Poem

Ask students what signs they see in the fall that help them know autumn has
arrived. Then ask students to think about how the poet feels about this fall as
they listen to the poem.

Introduce the Vocabulary

Write the vocabulary words on the board. Have partners alphabetize the
words, find the definitions in a dictionary, and record the meanings.
Challenge students to write sentences with the words.

During Reading

Read the poem aloud to students.

After Reading

Questions

1. What season does the poet write about? (*autumn*)
2. What does the poet compare the caterpillars to? (*snowmen*)
3. What examples of personification are in the poem? (*The wind wears
   sandals. The caterpillars wear winter coats. The trees have hands with fingers
   that flutter. The wind is a he that makes no noise. The frost tiptoes.*)
4. Does the poet want autumn to go? How do you know? (*She does not want
   autumn to go because she says, "Don't let the frost tiptoe into my ring on the
   magic grass," which means she wants to keep the cold out.*)

Fluency

Explain to students that that some lines in a poem do not have ending
marks. Point out that they should continue reading on the next line without
pausing. Then model reading an example from the poem with a pause and
without. Ask students which makes sense. Have students practice similar
sentences to develop fluency.

Develop Oral Language

Guide students to understand that the content of the poem often gives a clue
how to read it. Discuss how the poet feels about the season. Then challenge
students to read the poem as if they were the poet.

Writing

Review examples of personification in the poem. Then invite students to
write and illustrate their own examples of personification.

Autumn Song
by Hilda Conkling

I made a ring of leaves
On the autumn grass:
I was a fairy queen all day.
Inside the ring, the wind wore sandals
Not to make a noise of going.
The caterpillars, like little snow men,
Had wound themselves in their winter coats.
The hands of the trees were bare
And their fingers fluttered.
I was a queen of yellow leaves and brown,
And the redness of my fairy ring
Kept me warm.
For the wind blew near,
Though he made no noise of going,
And I hadn't a close-made wrap
Like the caterpillars.
Even a queen of fairies can be cold
When summer has forgotten and gone!
Keep me warm, red leaves;
Don't let the frost tiptoe into my ring
On the magic grass!

Autumn Song: Assessment

Think about the poem. Then answer the questions. Fill in the circle next to the correct answer.

1. What does the poet pretend to be?
- Ⓐ a fairy queen
- Ⓑ a caterpillar
- Ⓒ the wind

2. Which season left before the poet wrote this poem?
- Ⓐ winter
- Ⓑ summer
- Ⓒ spring

3. The "winter coats" of the caterpillars would be
- Ⓐ sweaters.
- Ⓑ cocoons.
- Ⓒ leaves.

4. This poem is mostly about
- Ⓐ pretending to be a fairy.
- Ⓑ how autumn feels.
- Ⓒ how caterpillars stay warm.

5. The poet was probably
- Ⓐ playing with friends.
- Ⓑ being punished.
- Ⓒ playing alone.

6. You can tell that the poet
- Ⓐ wants to be a caterpillar.
- Ⓑ does not want to be cold.
- Ⓒ believes that fairies are real.

7. Why did the poet get cold?

_____

_____

Name _____ Date _____

Troublesome Words

Some words sound alike, but they have different spellings and meanings.

  Example: Wanda **won one** race.

  won – to have done better than others in a race

  one – the number 1

🪶———— **Read the words in dark print. Write the form of the word that correctly completes each sentence.**

bare   bear

1. We looked through the branches of the _____ trees.

2. We saw a mother _____ and her cub.

blew   blue

3. Where is Rosa's _____ hat?

4. The wind _____ it away.

red   read

5. Miss Young posted a sign on _____ paper.

6. The students _____ the sign to find out what it said.

there   they're   their

7. _____ ready to leave now.

8. Where did Mr. Sims put _____ coats?

9. He put them over _____ by the door.

The Gardener

Poetry Skill: Rhyming Words

Standard
Identify rhyme

Explore Rhyming Words
The use of rhyming couplets will help students develop an understanding of rhyming words. Have students find the rhyming word pairs and circle them using matching crayon colors. Ask students which pair does not rhyme. Then have students choose one of the word pairs and brainstorm other words that rhyme with that pair.

Vocabulary

bare–empty or without covering
barrow–wheelbarrow
currant–berry bush
pinching–squeezing with the fingers
plots–garden areas
profit–to gain
serious–not silly
walk–path around a house or garden

Teacher Tips

"The Gardener" was written in the 1800s, so the language will be unfamiliar to students. Take the time to introduce the concept of *Cook* as it relates to life long ago.

Summary

Writing from a young boy's perspective, the poet describes a gardener who is serious and quiet.

Read the Poem

Introduce the Poem
Distribute the KWL chart on page 9 and have students write information that they know about gardens. When they are finished, have students share their responses. Then have students write questions about what they would like to know about gardens. As students read the poem, have them complete the last column in the chart to show other information they learned.

Introduce the Vocabulary
Write sentences on the board using the vocabulary words. Read the sentences and challenge students to guess the definitions. Discuss each answer, explaining how context would show that the guess was correct. After the definition is learned, have students suggest other sentences using the words.

During Reading

Ask a volunteer to read the poem.

After Reading

Questions
1. What kind of person is the gardener? (*Possible answer: He is very quiet but is a hard worker.*)
2. In what season does the poem take place? (*summer*)
3. Why does the poet think the gardener would be wiser to play games? (*Possible answer: The poet thinks the gardener is too serious and works too hard. He thinks the man is not having much fun.*)

Fluency
Direct students to find the sentence *Silly gardener!* Lead students in a discussion of how the poet might feel when he says the sentence and what tone he would use. Have students rehearse the poem, reading *Silly gardener!* with the appropriate expression.

Develop Oral Language
Working in groups of five, have each student choose and read one verse.

Writing

Ask students to choose a person to describe. Have them complete a concept web on page 10 to list adjectives to describe the person. Then invite students to write a paragraph or poem about the person using some words from their web. Challenge students who write poems to make some of the lines rhyme.

Name _____   Date _____

The Gardener
by Robert Louis Stevenson

The gardener does not love to talk.
He makes me keep the gravel walk;
And when he puts his tools away,
He locks the door and takes the key.

Away behind the currant row,
Where no one else but Cook may go,
Far in the plots, I see him dig,
Old and serious, brown and big.

He digs the flowers, green, red, and blue,
Nor wishes to be spoken to.
He digs the flowers and cuts the hay,
And never seems to want to play.

Silly gardener! Summer goes,
And winter comes with pinching toes,
When in the garden bare and brown
You must lay your barrow down.

Well now, and while the summer stays,
To profit by these garden days
O how much wiser you would be
To play at Indian wars with me!

Name _____   Date _____

The Gardener: Assessment

Think about the poem. Then answer the questions. Fill in the circle next to the correct answer.

1. What does the child in the poem want to do?
   Ⓐ dig in the garden
   Ⓑ play with other children
   Ⓒ play with the gardener

2. After the gardener puts his tools away,
   Ⓐ he plays with the child.
   Ⓑ he locks the door.
   Ⓒ he works in the garden.

3. The gardener is "old and serious." "Serious" means
   Ⓐ not joking.
   Ⓑ not healthy.
   Ⓒ not fast.

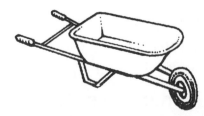

4. This poem is mostly about
   Ⓐ the cook.
   Ⓑ the flowers in the garden.
   Ⓒ the man who keeps the gardens.

5. You can tell that the gardener
   Ⓐ works hard at his job.
   Ⓑ does not like children.
   Ⓒ likes to play.

6. If the gardener played during the summer, it is likely that
   Ⓐ the cook would take care of the garden.
   Ⓑ the food and flowers would not grow.
   Ⓒ he could do his gardening in the winter.

7. Do you think the gardener is friendly? Why or why not?

   _____

   _____

Explore More

Antonyms

Antonyms are words with opposite meanings

Examples: open—close   long—short   up—down

Read each sentence. Find a word in the box that means the opposite of the word in parentheses. Write the word on the line.

bare	big	down	far	loved	old	play	serious

1. The gardener did not like to (work) _____.

2. She was always very (silly) _____.

3. The gardener walked (up) _____ the road to her flower plot.

4. It was not too (near) _____ from the house.

5. The plot was very (small) _____.

6. The gardener spent all day digging around the (young) _____ plants.

7. The neighbors knew that she (hated) _____ to be in the garden.

8. Even in the winter when the plants were (covered) _____, the woman was digging in the dirt.

Who Has Seen the Wind?

Standard
Recognize the use of repetition

Explore Repetition
Repetition is a sound device in which sounds, words, or phrases are repeated to emphasize a point. As students read the poem, ask them why the poet might repeat the phrase, *Who has seen the wind?*

Vocabulary

bow–to bend low from the waist
leaves–parts of a tree that help make food
neither–not
trembling–shaking
wind–moving air

Research Base

"When you immerse your students in rich, lively poetry, you introduce them to intense, concise, skillfully crafted language. They learn how authors convey a maximum amount of thought and feeling in the fewest, carefully chosen words. In a way, everything they need to know about reading and writing exists within a poem." (*Guiding Readers and Writers: Grades 3–6, p. 410*)

Summary

The poet tells how to look at trees to find out where the wind is.

Read the Poem

Introduce the Poem

Ask students if they have ever seen the wind. Then ask them how they know it is a windy day if they look out a window. Invite students to listen to a poem in which the poet describes how she can see the wind.

Introduce the Vocabulary

Write the vocabulary words on the board and ask volunteers to look up the words in a dictionary. Have the volunteer read all the definitions. Explain to students that some words have multiple meanings. Then have students read the poem to discover which meaning the words have in it.

During Reading

Ask volunteers to read the poem out loud.

After Reading

Questions

1. How are the two verses alike? (*The first line is the same in both verses.*)
2. How do the words change in the second line of each verse? Why? (*"I" and "you" are changed so that the poet can describe two images that will rhyme with each ending word.*)
3. What do you think the poet is comparing the trees to when she says, "When the trees bow down their heads"? (*She is comparing them to people.*)

Fluency

Help students explore how to read poems with line breaks that end in a semicolon. Write a semicolon on the board and explain that it means a reader should briefly pause, as when reading a period. Then model how to read the first verse with the semicolon and the unpunctuated line break. Ask students to practice reading the poem fluently.

Develop Oral Language

Invite pairs of students to record their version of the poem. Suggest they take turns making background wind sounds while reading with fluency and expression.

Writing

Distribute the Venn diagram on page 12, along with copies of "Who Has Seen the Wind?" and "The March Wind" on page 55 to pairs of students. Have them compare and contrast the poems to tell how the poets describe the wind.

Name _____   Date _____

Who Has Seen the Wind?
by Christina Rossetti

Who has seen the wind?
Neither I nor you;
But when the leaves hang trembling
The wind is passing through.

Who has seen the wind?
Neither you nor I;
But when the trees bow down their heads
The wind is passing by.

Lesson 15 • **Who Has Seen the Wind?:** Poem
Poetry: Grade 3, SV 9893-0

Name _____   Date _____

Who Has Seen the Wind?: Assessment

Think about the poem. Then answer the questions.
Fill in the circle next to the correct answer.

1. What is NOT talked about in the poem?
   Ⓐ leaves
   Ⓑ trees
   Ⓒ grass

2. When the wind passes through, the leaves
   Ⓐ tremble.
   Ⓑ dance.
   Ⓒ fall.

3. In the poem, "bow" means
   Ⓐ a tool used to shoot arrows.
   Ⓑ the front part of a ship.
   Ⓒ to bend.

4. Which sentence best tells what the poem is about?
   Ⓐ Trees lose their leaves.
   Ⓑ A person asks, "Who has seen the wind?"
   Ⓒ Although you can't see the wind, you know it's there by watching trees.

5. The poet knows the wind is around because she
   Ⓐ sees something move.
   Ⓑ feels it.
   Ⓒ hears it.

6. Why did the author write the poem?
   Ⓐ to tell about trees
   Ⓑ to describe the wind
   Ⓒ to write about a windy day

7. What season do you think is being described in the poem? How do you know?

_____

_____

Name _____ Date _____

Homographs

Homographs are words that have the same spelling but different meanings. Sometimes they may have different pronunciations. Use words in the sentence to help you choose the correct meaning of a word.

Example: bat
Meaning A: a kind of animal that flies
Meaning B: a toy that hits a ball

Circle the word that will correctly complete both sentences.

1. Mrs. Gonzales _____ for work at nine o'clock each morning.
   Autumn is the time that _____ fall off the trees.

   nuts   calls   leaves

2. You can _____ the key on the toy to make it move.
   The _____ is blowing too hard to fly the kite.

   wind   breeze   lift

3. Partners _____ to each other when they square-dance.
   Nancy shoots arrows with a _____.

   skip   bow   toy

4. The bus picks up the students and _____ to school.
   The puppies fell asleep with their _____ close together.

   paws   drives   heads

LESSON 16

The Eagle

Vocabulary

azure–blue
clasps–holds
crag–a rock that sticks out from a rocky wall
crooked–bent
thunderbolt–lightning
wrinkled–with lots of little folds

Research Base

"**Poetry** is a microcosm for learning. Through the precise, concise language of poetry, students learn a lot about reading and writing." (*Guiding Readers and Writers: Grades 3–6, p. 421*)

Summary

The poet describes an eagle.

Read the Poem

Introduce the Poem

Distribute the KWL chart on page 9 and have students write information that they know about eagles. When they are finished, have students share their responses. Allow them time to write questions about what they would like to know about eagles. Then as students read the poem, have them complete the last column in the chart.

Introduce the Vocabulary

Write the vocabulary words and the definitions on the board. Lead students in a brief discussion of the words. Then have students create a crossword puzzle with the words using the graph on page 11. Challenge students to write sentences as clues to complete the puzzle.

During Reading

Read the poem aloud to students.

After Reading

Questions

1. What does the poet mean when he says the eagle is close to the sun? (*The eagle is very high up on the mountain.*)
2. What is the "azure world"? (*the blue sky*)
3. Why might the eagle fall from its place on the mountain? (*Possible answer: It sees a fish or something it wants to eat.*)

Fluency

Point out that many poems have a rhythm, or beat. Then model how to read the poem rhythmically. Have students practice reading the poem to develop fluency.

Develop Oral Language

Have students retell the poem in their own words.

Writing

Have students circle the adjectives, or describing words, in the poem. Then have them choose a favorite animal to write a paragraph or a poem about. Challenge them to use at least four adjectives in their writing.

Name _____   Date _____

The Eagle
by Alfred, Lord Tennyson

He clasps the crag with crooked hands;
Close to the sun in lonely lands,
Ring'd with the azure world, he stands.

The wrinkled sea beneath him crawls;
He watches from his mountain walls,
And like a thunderbolt he falls.

Name _____   Date _____

The Eagle: Assessment

Think about the poem. Then answer the questions. Fill in the circle next to the correct answer.

1. Where is the eagle?
Ⓐ in the sea
Ⓑ in the sky
Ⓒ on a mountain

2. What does the eagle do after watching the sea?
Ⓐ He falls.
Ⓑ He calls.
Ⓒ He sleeps.

3. A "crag" is most likely
Ⓐ a cloud.
Ⓑ a rock.
Ⓒ a blade of grass.

4. This poem is mostly about
Ⓐ a mountain.
Ⓑ an eagle.
Ⓒ the sea.

5. The sea is probably called "wrinkled" because
Ⓐ it is moving.
Ⓑ it is old.
Ⓒ it is folded.

6. The eagle falls "like a thunderbolt" because
Ⓐ he is bright.
Ⓑ he is loud.
Ⓒ he is fast.

7. How do you know that "The Eagle" is a poem?

_____

_____

Troublesome Words

Some words sound alike, but they have different spellings and meanings.

> **Example:** I **ate eight** nuts.
> ate = chewed and swallowed food
> eight = the number 8

Read each sentence. Circle the words that sound alike. Then find the words in a dictionary. Write the meaning of each word.

1. Lea put the clothes in the suitcase and tried to close the lid.

_____

_____

2. Tim can see the sea from his hotel room.

_____

_____

3. Mrs. Wong's son went out to play in the sun.

_____

_____

4. Anna took off her ring to wring out the wet shirts.

_____

_____

A Bird's Home

Vocabulary

chirp–a quick sound a bird makes
feathered–covered in feathers
perched–sat on
sweetly–in a way that is pleasant or agreeable

Summary

Using a concrete poem format, the poet describes a bird's nest.

Read the Poem

Introduce the Poem

Have students look at the poem. Ask them what makes this poem different from other ones they have read. Lead students in a discussion of why a poet might make the words in a poem into a shape.

Introduce the Vocabulary

Write each word on a sentence strip, leaving spaces between each letter. Cut the letters apart and put the words into envelopes. Pass the envelopes out to groups and have students unscramble the letters to find the words. Discuss each word's meaning.

During Reading

Ask a volunteer to read the poem.

After Reading

Questions

1. What is a bird's home called? (*a nest*)
2. Who is speaking in the poem? (*the nest*)
3. What makes this poem fun to read? (*The poem is about a nest and the sentences are in the shape of a nest.*)

Fluency

Model how to read the poem rhythmically. Then invite students to rehearse the lines several times to become rhythmic readers.

Develop Oral Language

Invite students to read the poem chorally.

Writing

Invite students to choose another object and write a concrete poem about it to describe how it looks.

Name _____ Date _____

A Bird's Home
by Margaret Fetty

I am a home to feathered things,
Made of sticks and grass and string,
From here they chirp and sweetly sing,
And babies learn to flap their wings.
Perched on me, they are the kings.
I am a home to feathered things.

Name _____   Date _____

A Bird's Home: Assessment

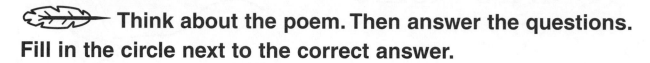 **Think about the poem. Then answer the questions. Fill in the circle next to the correct answer.**

1. What is the home made out of?
- Ⓐ sticks, grass, and mud
- Ⓑ sticks, grass, and string
- Ⓒ sticks, mud, and string

2. When do babies learn to flap their wings?
- Ⓐ before they fly
- Ⓑ before they eat
- Ⓒ before they break open the egg

3. What is the poet talking about when using the phrase "feathered things"?
- Ⓐ fans
- Ⓑ hats
- Ⓒ birds

4. Another title for the poem could be
- Ⓐ The Bird King.
- Ⓑ Singing Birds.
- Ⓒ A Nest.

5. The poet describes something that happens in the
- Ⓐ winter.
- Ⓑ fall.
- Ⓒ spring.

6. Birds probably sweetly sing when they are
- Ⓐ happy.
- Ⓑ flying.
- Ⓒ scared.

7. How is this poem different from other poems?

_____

_____

Synonyms

A synonym is a word that means the same or almost the same as another word.

Examples: start — begin   happy — glad

Read each sentence. Find a word in the box that means the same or almost the same as the word in dark print. Write the word on the line.

| carried   chirp   home   gently   made   small   sticks   string |

1. Ryan heard a soft **tweet**. _____

2. He looked under a tree and saw a **little** bird. _____

3. "You fell out of your **house**," said Ryan. _____

4. Ryan got some **yarn**. _____

5. He gathered some **twigs** and grass. _____

6. He **built** a nest inside a box to keep the bird safe. _____

7. Ryan **carefully** put the baby bird in the box. _____

8. Then he **took** the bird to a neighbor who helped baby animals. _____

To a Butterfly

Poetry Skill: Rhyming Words

Standard
Identify rhyme

Explore Rhyming Words
Remind students that some poems use rhyming words. Then have students find the rhyming words and circle them using matching crayon colors. Discuss the pattern of rhyming words in the poem.

Vocabulary

bough–tree branch
childish–like a child
lodge–to live
motionless–not moving
sanctuary–a safe place
self-poised–balanced by itself
weary–tired

Research Base

"To appreciate poetry is to appreciate the art of language." *(Guiding Readers and Writers: Grades 3–6, p. 410)*

Summary

The poet, seeing a butterfly, welcomes it into the safety of his orchard as he reflects on the carefree days of his youth.

Read the Poem

Introduce the Poem

Explain that some things stand for, or symbolize, a special concept. Discuss the symbols of a turkey (Thanksgiving), the United States flag (America and freedom), and other obvious symbols. Then ask students what the butterfly might symbolize. Ask students to listen to what the butterfly symbolizes for one poet.

Introduce the Vocabulary

Write the vocabulary words and the definitions on the board. Lead students in a brief discussion of the words. Then have students create a crossword puzzle with the words using the graph on page 11. Challenge students to write sentences as clues to complete the puzzle.

During Reading

Read the poem to students.

After Reading

Questions

1. Where is the poet? (*in an orchard*)
2. What does the poet compare the motionless butterfly to? (*frozen seas*)
3. Does the poet like to think about his youth? Why or why not? (*Yes, he likes to think about his youth because he wants to talk about and remember it.*)
4. What does the butterfly symbolize for the poet? (*the happy days of his childhood*)

Fluency

Explain that expression is how something is read. It includes the tone of the voice and speed of reading. Then discuss the mood of the poet and how it would influence expression. Invite partners to rehearse reading the poem using appropriate expression.

Develop Oral Language

Challenge students to retell the poem in their own words.

Writing

Ask students to think of something that is an important symbol to them. Have them draw a picture of it and write a paragraph or a poem to tell what it symbolizes.

Name _____   Date _____

To a Butterfly
by William Wordsworth

I've watched you now a full half-hour,
Self-poised upon that yellow flower,
And, little Butterfly! indeed
I know not if you sleep or feed.
How motionless!—not frozen seas
More motionless! and then
What joy awaits you, when the breeze
Hath found you out among the trees,
And calls you forth again!

This plot of orchard-ground is ours;
My trees they are, my Sister's flowers;
Here rest your wings when they are weary;
Here lodge as in a sanctuary!
Come often to us, fear no wrong;
Sit near us on the bough!
We'll talk of sunshine and of song,
And summer days, when we were young;
Sweet childish days, that were as long
As twenty days are now.

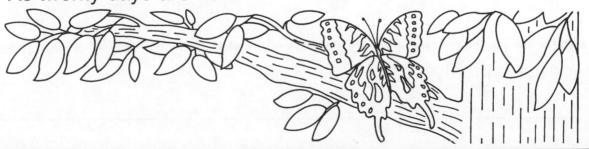

Name _____   Date _____

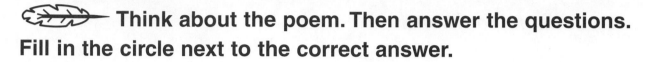
To a Butterfly: Assessment

Think about the poem. Then answer the questions. Fill in the circle next to the correct answer.

1. Who owns the orchard?
- Ⓐ the poet's sister
- Ⓑ the poet and his sister
- Ⓒ the poet's parents

2. What happens first?
- Ⓐ The breeze blows.
- Ⓑ The butterfly sits still.
- Ⓒ The butterfly lands on a flower.

3. The butterfly was motionless. "Motionless" means
- Ⓐ not pretty.
- Ⓑ not moving.
- Ⓒ not alive.

4. The poet is mostly saying
- Ⓐ he does not know what the butterfly is doing.
- Ⓑ he wants to talk to the butterfly.
- Ⓒ he wants the butterfly to feel safe in the orchard.

5. The poet probably
- Ⓐ enjoys nature.
- Ⓑ has a butterfly collection.
- Ⓒ misses his sister.

6. The poet seems to
- Ⓐ wish he were older.
- Ⓑ miss his younger days.
- Ⓒ want to be a butterfly.

7. Where is the poet in the poem? Why is this place a safe place for the butterfly?

_____

_____

Name _____   Date _____

Suffixes

A suffix is a small word part added to the end of a root word that changes the word's meaning.

Root Word	Suffix	Meaning	Example
hope	ful	full of	hopeful
motion	less	without	motionless
child	ish	in a certain way	childish

Read each sentence. Underline each word that has a suffix. Tell the meaning of the word. Use a dictionary if you need to.

1. Juan was cheerful as he sat in his backyard.

Meaning: _____

2. He saw a yellowish butterfly near him.

Meaning: _____

3. He thought it was beautiful.

Meaning: _____

4. The butterfly looked so helpless and weak.

Meaning: _____

5. It fluttered among the flowers under the cloudless sky.

Meaning: _____

The Feeder

Poetry Skill: Rhythm

Standard
Identify rhythm

Explore Rhythm
Explain to students that many poems have a specific rhythm, or beat. Then read the first verse of the poem and clap the beat as you read. Read the entire poem and ask students to clap the beat.

Vocabulary

feeder–a place to put food from which animals can eat
hues–colors
palette–a thin board used by artists to mix paints
timid–shy

Summary

Many different animals visit the poet's feeder.

Read the Poem

Introduce the Poem

In advance, obtain a bird book and mark the pages showing pictures of the birds identified in the poem. Before reading the poem, display the pictures and write the birds' names on the board. Read the poem title and ask students what the poem might be about.

Introduce the Vocabulary

Write the vocabulary words on the board. Have partners alphabetize the words, find the definitions in a dictionary, and record the meanings. Challenge students to write sentences with the words.

During Reading

Invite volunteers to read the poem.

After Reading

Questions

1. Why do you think the poet keeps the feeder near the window? (*So she can watch the birds and other animals that visit it.*)
2. What do the jays eat? (*sunflower seeds*)
3. The poet says that the cardinal is shy. What might the bird do at the feeder to show that he is shy? (*Answers will vary.*)
4. What might happen if the poet stopped feeding the birds? (*The birds would not come to her house anymore, and they would look for food in other places.*)

Fluency

Have children practice saying the names of the birds so they read the poem with smoothness and automaticity.

Develop Oral Language

Divide the class into four groups. Assign each group a verse. Have group members rehearse it so they can recite it chorally.

Writing

Explain that many poems use metaphors, a way to compare two things that are quite different. Then have students reread the line "The feeder is a palette." Discuss why the poet might use this comparison. Then challenge students to think of other things to compare. Have them write several metaphors.

The Feeder
by Thomasin Heyworth

The feeder by my window
Is a very busy spot.
It is when I am looking
And must be when I am not,
Because when I come
 back again
So many seeds are gone
That I know the birds have
 eaten them
(Or the squirrel that's on
 my lawn).

Chickadees and cardinals,
Nuthatches and jays,
I see them at the feeder
At different times of day.
The jays want only
 sunflower seeds;
They throw the rest about.
(The squirrel doesn't
 mind for he will eat
Whatever jay throws out.)

The cardinal is so bright red,
But he's a timid fellow.
Finches show up for a bite,
Showing off their yellow.
Chickadees, brown, black,
 and white,
Jays of brightest blues,
The feeder is a palette
Of nature's many hues.

I love to watch the feeder,
My cat enjoys it too!
(But I keep her away
 from there;
I know what she would do!)
I keep the feeder full of seeds
And watch the birds all year.
I give them the food they need,
And they keep stopping here!

Name _____   Date _____

The Feeder: Assessment

🪶 **Think about the poem. Then answer the questions. Fill in the circle next to the correct answer.**

1. What animals are in the poem?
   - Ⓐ birds and a squirrel
   - Ⓑ a squirrel and a cat
   - Ⓒ birds, a squirrel, and a cat

2. After the poet has been gone, she sees
   - Ⓐ the squirrel on the feeder.
   - Ⓑ many seeds are gone.
   - Ⓒ the cat is by the feeder.

3. The poem says, "The feeder is a palette/Of nature's many hues." "Hues" are
   - Ⓐ birds.
   - Ⓑ paints.
   - Ⓒ colors.

4. This poem is mostly about
   - Ⓐ birds.
   - Ⓑ cats.
   - Ⓒ squirrels.

5. You can tell that the squirrel
   - Ⓐ is afraid of the birds.
   - Ⓑ is a picky eater.
   - Ⓒ likes to eat the seeds.

6. The poet does not let the cat near the feeder because it
   - Ⓐ would play with the birds.
   - Ⓑ could hurt the birds.
   - Ⓒ would eat all the seeds.

7. Where do you think the poet lives?

_____

_____

Explore More

Words in Context

Use other words in sentences to help you find the missing word.

___

Read each sentence. Find a word from the box to complete it. Then write the word on the line.

| feeder | gift | hues | nature | palette | squirrel | timid | window |

1. Ross looked out the _____ into his backyard.

2. He had put seed in the _____ that morning.

3. Birds of many different _____ perched on it.

4. Even a _____ with a big bushy tail sat on a nearby tree branch.

5. It was not _____ as it tried to scare the birds away.

6. Ross thought all the plants and animals would make a wonderful painting that showed the outside beauty of

   _____.

7. He decided to get out his _____, paints, and brushes.

8. Ross would give the painting as a _____ to his mother for her birthday.

Poetry: Grade 3, SV 9893-0

The Little Mouse

Poetry Skill: Rhyming Words

Standard
Identify rhyme

Explore Rhyming Words
The use of rhyming couplets will help students develop an understanding of rhyming words. Have students find the rhyming word pairs and circle them using matching crayon colors. Then have students choose one of the word pairs and brainstorm other words that rhyme with that pair.

Vocabulary

creep–to walk slowly and quietly
daintiest–the freshest and prettiest to eat
hearty–big and filling
larder–a food closet
peep–to look secretly through a hole
spoiling–hurting food so that it cannot be eaten
venture–to go out, even if there is danger
wainscot–wood that covers part of a wall

Teacher Tips

"The Little Mouse" was written long ago, so the language and structure may confuse students. You may wish to read each line and challenge students to offer a translation.

Summary

The writer talks about a mouse's adventures in the house in this Mother Goose poem.

Read the Poem

Introduce the Poem

Invite students to share what they know about mice. Then tell students that they will read a poem that talks about a mouse that lives in a house.

Introduce the Vocabulary

In advance, write each letter of a word on separate cards. Put the letter cards for a word into an envelope. During class, write the vocabulary words on the board and share the definitions. Pass out the envelopes to small groups and have them unscramble the word. Then ask group members to use their word in a sentence. Have students identify the two words that rhyme.

During Reading

Read the poem aloud to students.

After Reading

Questions

1. Where does the mouse in the poem live? (*in a house*)
2. What kind of fun does the mouse have? (*choosing the food it wants to eat in the kitchen*)
3. How does the writer feel about the mouse? (*The writer doesn't like the mouse because it spoils the food.*)
4. What kind of dainty food do you think the mouse would look for? (*Answers will vary but should include foods that a mouse would enjoy eating.*)

Fluency

Help students explore how to read poems with line breaks that end in either a comma or semicolon. Write both a comma and a semicolon on the board. Explain that both punctuations signal that a reader should briefly pause, as when reading a period. Then model how to read the last six lines of the poem. Ask students to rehearse the same lines to develop fluency.

Develop Oral Language

Have partners reread the poem and alternate reading each couplet.

Writing

Have students draw a picture of their favorite part of the poem. Then have them rewrite the words of the poem into a sentence.

Lesson 20 • The Little Mouse: Teacher Information
Poetry: Grade 3, SV 9893-0

Name _____   Date _____

The Little Mouse
by Mother Goose

I have seen you, little mouse,
Running all about the house,
Through the hole your little eye
In the wainscot peeping sly,
Hoping soon some crumbs to steal,
To make quite a hearty meal.
Look before you venture out,
See if pussy is about.
If she's gone, you'll quickly run
To the larder for some fun;
Round about the dishes creep,
Taking into each a peep,
To choose the daintiest that's there,
Spoiling things you do not care.

Lesson 20 • **The Little Mouse:** Poem
Poetry: Grade 3, SV 9893-0

Understand the Poem

The Little Mouse: Assessment

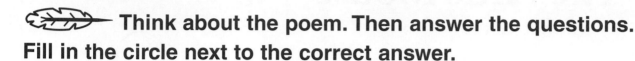 **Think about the poem. Then answer the questions. Fill in the circle next to the correct answer.**

1. What does the mouse want?
   Ⓐ to tease the cat
   Ⓑ to play with the poet
   Ⓒ to find some food

2. Before the mouse comes out,
   Ⓐ he looks for the cat.
   Ⓑ he goes to the larder.
   Ⓒ he steals some crumbs.

3. "Hearty" probably means
   Ⓐ stolen.
   Ⓑ filling.
   Ⓒ crunchy.

4. This poem is mostly about
   Ⓐ a cat looking for a mouse.
   Ⓑ a mouse looking for a friend.
   Ⓒ a mouse looking for a meal.

5. The mouse looks for the cat because
   Ⓐ the cat will steal food from the mouse.
   Ⓑ the cat will help the mouse find food.
   Ⓒ the cat will try to catch the mouse.

6. You can tell that the person in the poem
   Ⓐ does not want the mouse in the food.
   Ⓑ has a house with many mice in it.
   Ⓒ does not want the mouse to see the cat.

7. Why would the mouse look for the cat before leaving its hole?

_____

_____

Name _____ Date _____

Homographs

Homographs are words that have the same spelling but different meanings. Use words in the sentence to help you choose the correct meaning of a word.

Example: bat
Meaning A: a kind of animal that flies
Meaning B: a toy that hits a ball

Read each sentence. What does the word in dark print mean? Write the letter for the meaning of the word.

peep
Meaning A: to look secretly through a hole
Meaning B: the sound a baby chick makes

_____ **1.** We knew that the egg had hatched when we heard the chick's **peep**.

_____ **2.** Meg wanted to **peep** through the hole in the fence.

round
Meaning A: shaped like a ball
Meaning B: around

_____ **3.** A tire is **round**.

_____ **4.** The students ran **round** to the other side of the park.

run
Meaning A: to move faster than a walk
Meaning B: to work

_____ **5.** Mr. Carlson makes sure that the cars **run** well.

_____ **6.** Lee is going to **run** in a race.

Poetry Grade 3 • Answer Key

Page 8
1. C
2. A
3. C
4. B
5. C
6. A
7. Possible answer: The poet is describing things he saw at night before falling asleep when he was young.

Page 16
1. C
2. A
3. B
4. A
5. C
6. A
7. The poet must like rain because the poet describes it in a fun way.

Page 17
1. raindrops
2. overhead
3. sunbeam
4. thunderstorm
5. playground
Check that students' drawings reflect the meaning of each compound word.

Page 20
1. B
2. C
3. A
4. C
5. B
6. A
7. A limerick has an "aabba" rhyming pattern, and it has a special rhythm.

Page 21
1. happiest; most happy
2. joyful; full of joy
3. quickly; in a quick way
4. Suddenly; in a sudden way
5. forgetful; able to forget
6. longest; most in length

Page 24
1. C
2. A
3. B
4. A
5. B
6. C
7. The poet is comparing dancers at a party, also called a ball, with a soccer ball that people kick.

Page 25
Possible sentences given.
1. eye; People can wink with an eye.
2. wing; A wing is part of a bird that helps it fly.
3. trunk; Open the car trunk to put in the suitcase.
4. teeth; A dog can use its teeth to bite.
5. hands; People use hands to hold things.
6. bark; That dog bark sounds mean.

Page 28
1. A
2. C
3. A
4. B
5. B
6. B
7. It is winter because there are ice and snow on the ground.

Page 29
1. Emile didn't have a pet.
2. "I'll ask Dad if I can have a kitten," he said.
3. "That's a great idea!" said Mr. Sosa.
4. "But you'll have to take good care of the kitten," he added.
5. "Let's go to the pet shelter now," said Emile.
6. "We'll find the perfect kitten there!" he exclaimed.

Page 32
1. B
2. A
3. C
4. A
5. B
6. C
7. Possible answer: People who are in a bad mood are not nice. They might say and do things that hurt other people.

Page 33
1. large
2. scowl
3. shiver
4. perspire
5. gently
6. kiddies

Page 36
1. B
2. C
3. B
4. C
5. A
6. C
7. Most likely answer: There were so many things to count that she could not keep up with them all.

Page 37
1. vats
2. sloops
3. fleets
4. track
5. oodles
6. message
7. anxious
8. relief

Page 40
1. B
2. C
3. A
4. B
5. A
6. C
7. The person did not like the party because the person was very quiet. Most people who are quiet at a party may be uncomfortable.

Answer Key
Poetry: Grade 3, SV 9893-0

Poetry Grade 3 • Answer Key

Page 41
1. to and fro
2. voices
3. vying
4. least
5. feast
6. motions

Page 44
1. C
2. A
3. C
4. B
5. A
6. B
7. Possible answer: It does not rhyme, but the poem gives a picture of something in very few words. It has short lines and each line begins with a capital letter.

Page 45
1. ring
2. cookies
3. cars
4. circle
5. wall
6. sea

Page 48
1. C
2. B
3. A
4. B
5. C
6. A
7. Possible answers: The poet uses many words that relate to sailing as he talks about getting ready for bed and sleeping. He goes on "board," which means he is getting on the boat. He says goodnight to his friends on "shore," and he "sails away." He takes things that a "sailor" should. He and his toy "steer" through the dreams, and his "vessel" returns to the "pier."

Page 49
1. see–to look at
sea–ocean
2. sale–able to be bought
sail–moving across water using wind power
3. two–the number after 1
to–for the purpose of
4. bored–not interested
board–to get on a boat or airplane

Page 52
1. B
2. B
3. B
4. C
5. C
6. A
7. She sees things like flowers, cliffs, and the wind. She touches things like the flowers.

Page 53
1. B
2. A
3. B
4. A
5. B
6. A

Page 56
1. B
2. A
3. B
4. A
5. C
6. B
7. Most likely answer: The wind warms the air and soil, which warm the things that grow.

Page 57
1. rumble
2. crash
3. drip drop
4. bark
5. slam
6. crunched
7. knock
8. Boom

Page 60
1. B
2. C
3. C
4. C
5. C
6. A
7. Answers will vary. Accept reasonable answers.

Page 61
1. rust dust
2. mood food
3. heart tart
4. slow crow

Page 64
1. A
2. B
3. B
4. B
5. C
6. B
7. She was not wearing a heavy coat.

Page 65
1. bare
2. bear
3. blue
4. blew
5. red
6. read
7. They're
8. their
9. there

Page 68
1. C
2. B
3. A
4. C
5. A
6. B
7. Most likely answer: The gardener is not friendly because he doesn't want to be spoken to, and only Cook is allowed in the garden.

Poetry Grade 3 • Answer Key

Page 69
1. play
2. serious
3. down
4. far
5. big
6. old
7. loved
8. bare

Page 72
1. C
2. A
3. C
4. C
5. A
6. B
7. Accept reasonable answers of summer or fall.

Page 73
1. leaves
2. wind
3. bow
4. heads

Page 76
1. C
2. A
3. B
4. B
5. A
6. C
7. Possible answer: It gives a quick picture of what an eagle is doing. It is written with short, rhyming lines that have a special beat.

Page 77
1. clothes–things to wear
close–to shut
2. see–to look at
sea–ocean
3. son–a boy child
sun–the closest star to Earth
4. ring–a piece of jewelry that is often worn on a finger
wring–to twist

Page 80
1. B
2. A
3. C
4. C
5. C
6. A
7. The sentences not only describe a nest, but they form the nest shape, too.

Page 81
1. chirp
2. small
3. home
4. string
5. sticks
6. made
7. gently
8. carried

Page 84
1. B
2. C
3. B
4. C
5. A
6. B
7. The poet is in an orchard. It is a safe place because there are trees and flowers in which the butterfly can rest or from which it can feed.

Page 85
1. cheerful–full of cheer
2. yellowish–in a yellow way
3. beautiful–full of beauty
4. helpless–without help
5. cloudless–without clouds

Page 88
1. C
2. B
3. C
4. A
5. C
6. B
7. Possible answer: The poet lives in a rural area where there are squirrels, cats can roam, and there is a big backyard.

Page 89
1. window
2. feeder
3. hues
4. squirrel
5. timid
6. nature
7. palette
8. gift

Page 92
1. C
2. A
3. B
4. C
5. C
6. A
7. The cat might try to catch the mouse.

Page 93
1. B
2. A
3. A
4. B
5. B
6. A

Reference
Fountas, Irene C. and Pinnell, Gay Su. 2001. *Guiding Readers and Writers: Grades 3–6.* Portsmouth, NH: Heinemann.

Answer Key
Poetry: Grade 3, SV 9893-0